WALKS FOR ALL AGES
NORTH EAST WALES

WALKS *FOR* *ALL* AGES

NORTH EAST
WALES

JUDY SMITH

BRADWELL
BOOKS

Published by Bradwell Books
9 Orgreave Close Sheffield S13 9NP
Email: books@bradwellbooks.co.uk
© Judy Smith 2014

British Library Cataloguing in Publication Data: a catalogue record for this book is available from the British Library.

1st Edition

ISBN: 9781902674773

Print: Gomer Press, Llandysul, Ceredigion SA44 4JL
Design by: Erik Siewko Creative, Derbyshire.
eriksiewko@gmail.com

Photograph Credits: © Judy Smith 2014
Cover & page 5: North Wales Tourism

Maps: Contain Ordnance Survey data
© Crown copyright and database right 2014

Ordnance Survey licence number 100039353

The information in this book has been produced in good faith and is intended as a general guide. Bradwell Books and its authors have made all reasonable efforts to ensure that the details are correct at the time of publication. Bradwell Books and the author cannot accept any responsibility for any changes that have taken place subsequent to the book being published. It is the responsibility of individuals undertaking any of the walks listed in this publication to exercise due care and consideration for the health and wellbeing of themselves and others. Particular care should be taken if you are inexperienced. The walks in this book are not especially strenuous but individuals taking part should ensure they are fit and able to complete the walk before setting off.

CONTENTS

INTRODUCTION

THIS NORTH-EAST CORNER OF WALES IS A WONDERFUL AREA FOR WALKING. THE VERDANT DEE VALLEY, THE ROLLING SLOPES OF THE CLWYDIANS, THE WIDE SHORES OF THE NORTH AND THE DEE ESTUARY, AND THE LONELY WATERS OF LLYN BRENIG SET DEEP IN PINEWOODS WITH THE WILD BERWYNS AND DISTANT SNOWDONIA FOR BACKDROP, MAKE IT A RAMBLER'S PARADISE.

And walkers from far and wide flock here all year round. Needless to say, route information is abundant, and the shelves of Tourist Offices are groaning with the weight of walking books. So what makes this one different?

Well, maybe you are not a habitual walker. Although you enjoy a walk, perhaps pressure of work or the commitments of a young family mean you have little spare time to get out and about. And you don't have walking boots, or the oft-quoted 'Gore-tex and gaiters'. Whether you live in the area and want to explore more of it or are visiting on holiday, this book is for you. The walks here are simple and short, none of them longer than six miles. They don't venture into wild countryside, and for the most part can be managed quite comfortably in trainers. Both the instructions and the map for each route are very clear, so no great expertise in map-reading is needed. And almost all the walks either start from or visit a local beauty spot or feature of interest. Castles, waterfalls, abbeys, heritage sites, a beach, a mountain, a stately home and more are here – you could even think of this book as a mini-guide to the area. But having said all that, the real raison d'être is to offer excursions that are suitable for all the family, and for that reason every walk gives special consideration to the children. If the children are happy, then Mum and Dad, Grandma and Grandpa, and everyone else is too.

Children have boundless energy and most six- or seven-year-olds can easily outwalk their parents if they feel so inclined. The problem is to keep them interested. To that end, a walk should have a reason, and the walks in this book have all been designed to have some element of excitement and purpose

about them. Climbing above a waterfall, visiting a castle, exploring a lead mine, finding bullet holes from the Civil War, conquering a mountain (photograph obligatory!) and the like have obvious child-appeal. And should that not be enough, an extra 'Challenge', a sort of 'I-Spy' game, has been included with each walk. Usually there are just five or six things to spot on the way round, and, of course, all the family can join in this one. It's up to the adults to make sure there's a reward on hand for success!

All the specific information you need for each walk is set out at its beginning – and to add to the day's enjoyment, suggestions for picnic stops, ice cream shops en route and pubs and cafés where children are welcomed are included. So off you go – explore this lovely corner of Wales as a family.
Good luck on your journey!

Judy Smith

DYSERTH WATERFALL

Dyserth Waterfall and Graig Fawr

All around this north-east corner of Wales a limestone escarpment rises steeply behind the coastal plain, and at Dyserth the River Ffyddion takes a dramatic tumble over the sharp edge.

The Ffyddion isn't a great river – after all, it only rises a mere four miles from Dyserth – but the 70-foot drop is impressive nevertheless, and set amid mossy cliffs and the remains of one-time watermills, it makes a pretty scene.

This walk begins at the waterfall and from there climbs to the site known as Graig Fawr. Graig Fawr is just what its Welsh name implies: a huge rock, an outcrop projecting from the escarpment behind. At 153m (500 feet) it isn't the highest point around, but it does have a king-sized view encompassing Prestatyn and a long stretch of golden coast, the Berwyn Mountains to the south, and far-away Snowdonia.

Beneath your feet here is beautiful limestone grassland, alive with colourful wild flowers and butterflies in summertime. And much further beneath your feet, the rock is riddled with tunnels and caves, the relics of long-gone years of lead and copper mining. Graig Fawr is now in the care of the National Trust, having been donated by the steel magnate Sir Geoffrey Summers.

So here are two fascinating features in one very short walk, and you can add to those the site of the former Dyserth Castle, and nearby St Bridget's churchyard, where there are some rare Jacobean hooded tombs. Don't waste a moment – get out and see it all today!

FOR THE CHILDREN

- Waterfalls are always magic.
- The summit of Graig Fawr is surely a spot for a photograph; and running down the grassy slopes is fun.

Now for the Challenge! Can you spy a green bench, an old mangle, a horse, a church steeple, a seagull, a football goal (distant!), a monkey puzzle tree? Get them all? Fantastic!

THE BASICS

Distance: 3½ miles (5½km)

Gradient: Fairly steep just above the waterfall and at the foot of Graig Fawr

Severity: Moderate

Time: 2 hours

Stiles: 6

Map: OS Explorer 264, Vale of Clwyd

Path description: Grassy paths, tarmacked disused railway

Parking: At Dyserth Waterfall Grid Ref SJ 056792, LL18 6ET. Very small donation requested for entry to waterfall

Dogs: Dog-friendly. All stiles can be bypassed. The National Trust asks that dogs are on leads on Graig Fawr

Refreshment: Café beside the car park at the falls. Pubs nearby

Start Point: SJ 056792 or LL18 6ET

Toilets: At the Cafe and local Pubs

DYSERTH WATERFALL WALK

1. From the carpark follow the signs to the Waterfall. Go past the waterfall and continue on the path climbing to its summit. *The two high walls at the start of the walk are thought to belong to a former mill.* Pass the two viewpoint seats and drop down to a path junction with signpost. Turn left here, and continue over the first stile (ignore the path going right) and go on to a second stile at the end of the path.

2. Turn right on the road and follow it for some 400m to a T-junction. Go left, and just over a bridge (150m), turn right and then right again to pass under the bridge on a disused railway line. *The line was opened in 1869 initially to transport limestone from the quarries, although a passenger service soon followed. It closed in 1973.* Continue on the railway line for about half a mile (nearly 1km) until you see ahead the rails of another bridge. Leave the line here to go through  a gap in the stone wall on the right and climb to the road. A very short path now leads up the bank to a ladder stile entering the National Trust land of Graig Fawr.

3. Once over the stile, climb the steps to a fork in the path. All paths lead to the summit, but perhaps go left to a clearing and then right. You are soon on open grassy slopes with an obvious path leading up to the trig pillar with its most magnificent view.

4. When you are ready to leave, take the wide grassy path heading off in the direction of Prestatyn on the coast way below. The path curves gently right between clumps of gorse, and soon arrives at a marker post at the edge of the National Trust area. Go right here, soon passing along the edge of a wide field, then bearing left into a second field. Cross this one diagonally right, then, with a wooden entrance gate ahead, bear right again to descend gently to an exit kissing gate and car park beyond.

5. At the junction at the car park entrance take the road opposite, then in 15m turn right down a narrow lane marked 'Only for Access'. Continue down the lane for about 200m, then taking a footpath over a stile on the right. The path skirts a field, then bends right to a stile. After a second stile (beside a metal gate) the path forks. *Ahead here the path leads into a quarry above which was the one-time site of Dyserth Castle. This was an*

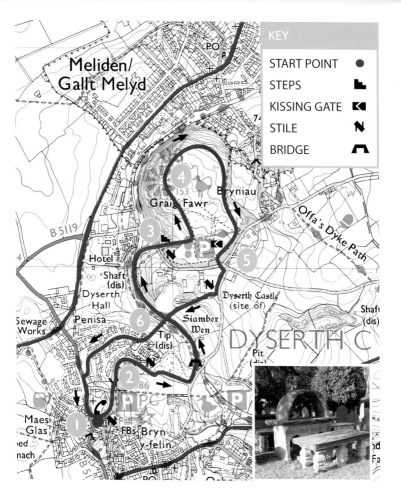

KEY

START POINT	●
STEPS	⬛
KISSING GATE	◄
STILE	Ν
BRIDGE	⌐

'English' castle, built by Henry III in the 13th century, but it survived for less than 20 years before being destroyed by the Welsh. Little evidence remains since the site was quarried. From the quarry return to the fork and take the other path, going downhill to pass through a gate under the railway line.

6. In the field ahead, cross the stream then bear right uphill to a path between garden fences. Reaching the road (Gwelfor Parc), go right and follow it as it bends left to descend to the main road. Turn left to return to the car park and Waterfall site. *On the way you pass St Bridget's church, renowned for its fine Jesse window. In the churchyard at the east end of the church are two late 17th-century hooded or canopied tombs, housing the remains of the Hughes of Llewerllyd family, who claimed descent from an 11th-century King of North Wales.*

TALACRE

ABOVE THE TIDE AT TALACRE

EVERYONE LOVES A WALK AT THE SEASIDE AND THE FIRM
GOLDEN SANDS OF TALACRE COULDN'T BE MORE PERFECT
FOR A FAMILY STROLL.

The wide beach here runs right up to the Point of Ayr, the spit of sand that marks the entrance to the Dee estuary – and although there may be some concession to holidaymakers in the village, that beach itself it is quite unspoiled, and flanked on its eastern side by a bird reserve.

Peaceful it may be today, but this is a beach with a history. In World War II fighter aircraft did their target practice here, and later the place

was frequently sprinkled with 'tin foil window' to test its anti-radar potential. A coal mine with a shaft under the beach was operational right up until 1996, and now a nearby plant processes natural gas received by pipeline from the Douglas Complex, 15 miles (24km) out to sea.

Fortunately neither war, nor industry, nor tourism has had an adverse effect on the beach and dunes here, and the area is now a Site of Special Scientific Interest (SSSI). The dunes are particularly important for their population of natterjack toads, which are rare in Britain. You will need to be here in the evening to see them, and should it also be springtime, you might be treated to a cacophony of loud mating calls as well.

The walk sets out on an easy path through these dunes, passing a toad conservation area before turning to reach the beach itself. At low tide, colonies of curlews and oystercatchers can often be seen across the sands – and don't forget to cast your eyes out to sea, where you may glimpse the bobbing heads of grey seals.

On the horizon all the way back is the lighthouse at the Point and you can walk right up to it most of the time, although at high tide it could be as much as 40m out at sea. The lighthouse was built in 1776, but became redundant in 1883 when it was replaced by a lightship. Since that time there have apparently been many ghostly sightings of the one-time lighthouse-keeper in long coat and hat!

Recently, someone saw fit to install a sculpture of a lighthouse-keeper made from plates of stainless steel on the gallery beside the light. For further effect, the wind blows through the gaps in the plates with an eerie whine. Could the real ghost have been frightened off?

FOR THE CHILDREN

- The beach is great for running, flying kites, and hunting for shells.
- The path through the dunes is good for bikes and pushchairs.
- Take a good look at that lighthouse. Is the ghost howling?
- There's no problem in finding an ice cream at the end of this walk – even on a January day!

And for the Challenge, can you spot a horse, a lighthouse logo on a disc, a picture of a rabbit, a whole razor shell (double), a flag, a boat at sea? Take a bonus for a seal (binoculars might help!), and a super-bonus for the lighthouse ghost (the real one!)

THE BASICS

Distance: 3 miles (5km) (can be reduced to 1¼ miles / 2km). To visit RSPB hide, extra half-mile (1km) each way

Gradient: A level walk

Severity: Easy

Time: 2 hours

Stiles: None

Map: OS Explorer 265, Clwydian Range

Path description: Hard-surfaced path, firm sand. It should be possible to walk on the beach on all but the highest tides, but you might like to check the tide table before you go (www.britishbeaches.info/point-of-ayr-talacre)

Parking: Car park next to Smugglers Inn near end of road. Grid Ref SJ 125848 or CH8 9RD

Toilets: On road before car park

Dogs: Welcome on beach at all times

Refreshment: Cafés and pubs in Talacre

Start Point: From the car park CH8 9RD

TALACRE WALK

1. From the car park walk up to the end of the road and, opposite the last café, turn left to go through a cycle barrier on to a metalled track (SP Gronant). Go over the boardwalk and at the junction, keep right for about 800m to a signed junction.

2. Here a path goes off to the right through the dunes – a short cut (turn right at the first junction and head towards the sea). To continue with the main route, keep ahead here, pass a fenced conservation area with obvious toad-friendly marsh, and continue to a barrier leading into a caravan site.

3. Take the first turning on the right (40m), then bend quickly left and right to reach a sign board at the entrance to the dunes. Continue on the boardwalk, and then on the sandy path over the dunes to the beach. *Ahead of you are two offshore wind-farms. The one on the left is North Hoyle, the first in the UK, instituted in 2003.* Turn right along the shore and after a few minutes' walking the lighthouse will come into view way ahead. When you reach it take time to admire it (and look out for the new 'keeper'), then go on up the beach for about 200m to where a red flag is flying.

4. Turn right here, cross a boggy patch, and climb to the viewing platform. Can anyone see Blackpool Tower? Continue along the metalled path, keeping ahead to a junction above the end of the road. *Here an extra half-mile (1km) walk will take you to the RSPB hide out on the marshes.* To return to the car park, go down to the road and turn left.

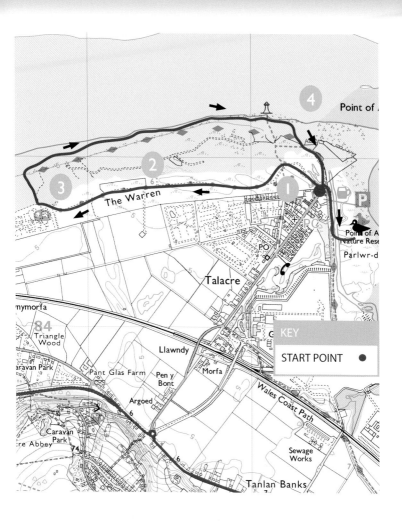

Point of A

Point of A
Nature Rese

Parlwr-d

The Warren

4

2

3

1

Talacre

PO

PC

P

nymorfa

84

Triangle
Wood

aravan Park

Llawndy

Morfa

Pant Glas Farm

Pen y
Bont

Argoed

Caravan
Park

re Abbey

74

Wales Coast Path

Sewage
Works

7

Tanlan Banks

KEY

START POINT ●

HOLYWELL

Monks and Mills at Holywell

ONCE UPON A TIME THERE WAS A LUSH GREEN VALLEY
WHERE A LITTLE STREAM TUMBLED FROM THE HEIGHTS
OF HALKYN MOUNTAIN TO THE REEDY SHORES OF THE
ESTUARY BELOW.

Then, in the 7th Century a miracle happened. Caradog,
son of a local prince, was forcing his attentions on the
young nun Winefride, who ran away from him up these
slopes. So angered was Caradog that he cut off her
head. Winefride's uncle, St Bueno, emerged from his
church nearby and promptly united head and body again.
A spring gushed from the ground where the head had
fallen – and from that moment the once-lonely valley became a busy scene of pilgrimage.

Some 500 years later, monks from Savigny in Normandy came here, and decided to build
themselves a new abbey on the lower slopes. They used that stream to power their corn

mill, and to treat wool from their sheep, and so they grew
rich. All this came to an end with Henry VIII's Dissolution
of the Monasteries in 1536.

Fast-forward 200 years again, and the potential of
Holywell Stream did not escape the pioneers of the
Industrial Revolution. First to be established were copper
and brass mills, 'battering' sheet metal into bowls and
pans. Then came a cotton mill and a copper rolling mill, all of them driven by the waters
of that stream. Mill usage changed over the years but by the early 20th century all

production had ceased, and the buildings of the valley soon fell into disrepair. Happily, that's not the end of the story. Some 30 years ago Flintshire County Council decided to adopt this neglected place, and open it for public recreation. From the handsome ruins of Basingwerk Abbey at the lower end, paths meander through all the old mill sites, now engulfed in vegetation again, and lead to St Winefride's Well at the top. 'Greenfield Valley' makes a fascinating short ramble, and at the end of it there's a Visitor Centre, a tea room, and even a Victorian farm for added interest.

FOR THE CHILDREN

- Millwheels and other old machinery are fascinating.
- You need a few pence to go into St Winefride's Well but it has all the atmosphere you might expect.
- There's a small entry fee at the Farm Museum as well, but it's worth it (open April to October).

And here's this walk's Challenge! Look out for a carving of a dragonfly, a mallard, a red lifebuoy, the date 1830 in Roman numerals (look behind you!), a red and white square on a post (an orienteering symbol), a bird box. Get all six and you are brilliant!

THE BASICS

Distance: 2½ miles (4km)

Gradient: Gentle climbs only

Severity: Easy

Time: 2 hours

Stiles: None

Map: OS Explorer 265, Clwydian Range. But we recommend to get a site map from the Visitor Centre as well

Parking: Car park on A548 Flint road. Grid ref SJ 196775 or CH8 7PN

Toilets: At Visitor Centre

Path description: Almost all on easy hard-surfaced tracks

Dogs: No stiles, but dogs will need to be on a lead

Refreshments: Tea room near the Visitor Centre (open April to October)

Start Point: From the car park, CH8 7PN

HOLYWELL WALK

1. Leave the car park at the top left corner, passing under the carved archway. Soon ruined Basingwerk Abbey is on your right (free entry through a kissing gate) and the Visitor Centre on your left. Turn left in front of the Old School (rebuilt here from nearby) and reaching the lane, keep  left. *On your right is a waterwheel that powered a copper wire factory.* After 200m approx, turn right down steps leading to the Lower Cotton Mill. *Dating from 1785, the mill was once a six-storey building employing more than 300 men. It became a corn mill in 1850, finally closing some 60 years later.*

   Retrace your steps to the lane and continue uphill to the big reservoir, Flour Mill Pool. The lane bears left here, but you continue beside the reservoir, bearing right at the big metal gates. *The ruins here are those of Meadow Mill – you will see them better from the walkway in a minute. The mill was built in 1787, producing copper rollers to print patterns on cloth. Later there was a rubber grinding works and a tin plate works on this huge site.* Bear left to go up steps, then turn right on to the metal walkway between mill site and another reservoir. At its end go up steps to a car park.

2. Leave the car park via a kissing gate near the road entrance. Pass a clock tower and immediately afterwards keep right, passing the remains of the old battery factory. *The battery works opened in 1776, producing copper pots and pans. Shipped to Africa, these goods were exchanged for slaves, who were in turn taken to the cotton fields of America. This 'triangular' trade was completed by bringing cotton back to Britain.* Continue beside Battery Pool, now drained, soon forking left on a lesser path to cut across the top of the Pool. The path emerges under a metal arch in the car park of the Royal Oak.

3. Go left up steps, then right on the lower of two paths. Continue 250m to a kissing gate, then bear right to descend to the road. Turn left for 200m to reach St Winefride's Well. *Pilgrims flocked to visit St Winifred's Well in the Middle Ages. Several monarchs are known to have come, among them Richard I (praying for his crusades), Henry V (giving thanks for Agincourt) and James II (seeking a male heir). The chapel over the well was built by Lady Margaret Beaufort (Henry VII's mother) in the 15th century. Pilgrims still come every day, and many bathe in the outside pool.*

4. Return to the kissing gate and now take the right upper path, a disused railway track. *Built in 1869 to transport rock from the quarries to the port, it found later use in delivering pilgrims to the Well.* Simply stay on this broad track, ignoring all

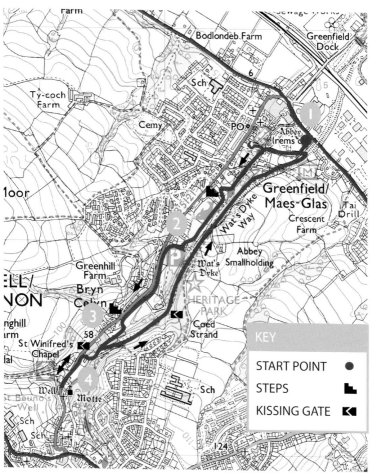

KEY

START POINT ●

STEPS ◣

KISSING GATE ◄◣

others, for about 700m. About 200m after crossing a small bridge, a strong track on the left doubles back to Basingwerk Abbey and all the amenities.

RIVER ELWY

St Asaph and the River Elwy

St Asaph Cathedral, the smallest such in England and Wales, sits on the last knoll of high ground in the Vale of Clwyd, looking out over wide plains that stretch to the sea.

Its history began in the 6th century when St Kentigern from Strathclyde founded a monastery nearby. When he returned to his native country, Asaph, his favoured disciple, took over the reins and, for some reason long forgotten, it is his name rather than Kentigern's that is commemorated by the city. In the 13th century, this early Christian edifice was replaced by a new church, which soon suffered at the hands of Henry I, Owain Glyndwr and others, but was built up yet again. It is this church that, with some later remodelling by Gilbert Scott in the 19th century, has become the cathedral of today. It must surely warrant a few moments of your time before you set off on this walk.

Below the cathedral the houses tumble down to the banks of the River Elwy, skirting the city on its way to join the Clwyd. The Elwy may not be much of a torrent under normal conditions, but since a rise in its level could soon cause flooding on the flat alluvial plain a substantial embankment has been built on its west side. Even that could not resist the heavy rainfall of November 2012, when hundreds of houses were flooded here. Nevertheless, it is that embankment that provides us with this exhilarating walk where on the one side you have the river, and on the other, low fields stretching into a far distance. The sea is only an ozone-breath away, gulls wheel over the meadows, and out there you

can spy the ruined turrets of Rhuddlan Castle above the trees, and the marble church at Bodelwyddan pointing an ivory needle to the sky. The return is on a quiet narrow lane running along the high ridge between the two rivers, and it offers yet more views. Across the Vale of Clwyd the land drops precipitately to the sea near Prestatyn, and immediately inland, the wooded slopes of Mynydd-y-Cwm herald the more lofty Clwydians to the south. Take your time to admire it all on this short walk.

FOR THE CHILDREN

- Good carefree running on the embankment. 'King of the Castle' effect!
- A short walk that could have the lure of a good playground at the end – and plenty of shops for ice cream!

And of course, the Challenge. There are a lot of numbers in this one! Can you spot the number 84, the number 51 and the date 1953? Add to those a picture of a heron (take a bonus for the real thing!), a convex mirror, and an effigy of a dog on a farm sign. If you get them all you are truly eagle-eyed!

THE BASICS

Distance: 3 miles (4.5km)
Gradient: Only one short gentle climb
Severity: Easy
Time: 2 hours
Stiles: 3
Map: OS Explorer 264, Vale of Clwyd
Path description: Grassy embankment, quiet lane, suburban pavement
Parking: St Asaph cathedral car park, Grid Ref SJ 039742 or LL17 0RD Alternatively, start at Point 2 if you want to take advantage of the riverside picnic area and playground
Toilets: At Point 2 also
Dogs: Dogs can run freely on embankment. All stiles are provided with dog gates
Refreshments: Several cafés and restaurants in St Asaph
Start Point: At the car park, LL17 0RD

RIVER ELWY WALK

1. From the car park walk across to the cathedral, then take the path running around its left-hand side. *The grave of the composer William Matthias (1934–92) is on the left as you go round. You might notice that the cathedral is built with some decidedly different types of stone – light limestone, yellowish sandstone from near Flint, and local purple sandstone.* Once round the cathedral continue down the steps (monument to the translators of the Welsh Bible on your right) and turn left down the High Street. At its lower end, cross the road towards the car park. *Here a twisted silver sculpture, topped by a Congolese figure, commemorates the explorer HM Stanley's links with the town. Born in Denbigh, he spent his early years in the workhouse at St Asaph.*

2. Continue over the bridge and turn right. In 40 metres, take a tarmacked path on the right running up to the embankment above the river. Now continue with the Elwy on your right, passing the cattle market and going under the A55. When the cycle track goes off left, keep ahead on the grassy bank to reach a kissing gate before a minor road

3. Cross this road directly and continue on the embankment. Pass through another kissing gate, then continue with views of Rhuddlan ahead. After a bend come two stiles with dog gates (the Marble Church clearly visible here), and just a little further on, steps lead down to a footbridge over the river.

4. Cross the bridge, go over a stile (again with dog gate) and turn right on the lane. After passing a large property on the left the lane climbs steeply to the summit of a ridge. *The Elwy is now on your right, the Clwyd on your left. Across the latter you can see the end of the Clwydians dipping to the sea.* Continue past an old farm and across the A55 bridge into the outskirts of town.

5. Where the road swings right, go ahead into Oak Lane, then immediately right between the cemetery wall and a fence. Bear right with this path to meet a road, turn left, and continue to the cathedral.

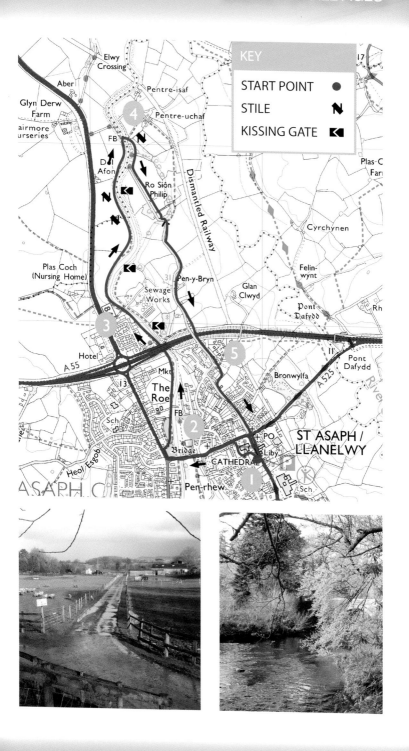

KEY

START POINT ●

STILE ↗

KISSING GATE ◄

DENBIGH

The Great and the Good in Denbigh

Whichever way you arrive in Denbigh you can't fail to be impressed by the castle. There it sits, all grey towers and crumbling walls, looking down on the town that sprawls at it's feet.

You can't come to Denbigh without visiting that castle – and you can't come to that castle without paying homage to Denbigh's famous son who was born at its gates. Henry Morton Stanley, journalist, African explorer and renowned finder of Livingstone, was born in a cottage long demolished but whose site is marked by a plaque. In truth, Stanley (then known as John Rowlands) lived only a mere six years in Denbigh before being shipped off to

the workhouse in St Asaph. That harsh upbringing was responsible for his lifelong diffidence, a shyness that rendered him tongue-tied when finally meeting Livingstone after eight months searching through the jungle. His 'Dr Livingstone, I presume' has gone down in history. A statue of Stanley, hand outstretched in greeting, stands outside Denbigh Library.

The walk here ends at the castle and library, but it begins by crossing fields to the lovely house of Gwaenynog, where there is more history. At one time it belonged to an uncle of Beatrix Potter, who stayed here many times. It is well known that the walled kitchen garden was the inspiration for her tale of the Flopsy Bunnies, and that the potting shed was Mr

McGregor's domain! A somewhat earlier visitor to Gwaenynog was Dr Samuel Johnson, the writer and dictionary compiler, and it seems that in 1774 he also stayed in a cottage on the estate. Now in ruins, that cottage is passed on this walk, which also visits the monument to Dr Johnson in his favourite field by the river.

Is this walk only about famous people? Maybe – but the countryside here is glorious too. All is set around the valley of the little River Ystrad where woods frame gentle riverside meadows that are just perfect for a picnic.

FOR THE CHILDREN

- Tell the children the story of Livingstone and Stanley – if they don't already know it!
- They probably do know the tale of the Flopsy Bunnies. It's a pity you can't see more of the garden on this walk, but you can imagine.
- Take a snack with you to enjoy in one of those fields by the river.

And the Challenge – can you spot the date 1995, a horse on a weather vane, horse jumps, a stone drinking trough, a bird table, a carving of an owl. You can? Brilliant!

THE BASICS

Distance: 5½ miles (9km)

Gradient: Gently undulating

Severity: Easy

Time: 3 hours

Stiles: 6

Map: OS Explorer 264, Vale of Clwyd

Path description: Woodland and field paths. Half a mile (1km) alongside road at end

Parking: Car parks near roundabout beside Hand Inn, Lenten Pool, Denbigh. Grid Ref SJ 050661 or LL16 3PF

Toilets: In the car park

Dogs: Not really dog-friendly, with impassable stiles and grazing livestock

Refreshments: Eating houses in the neighbourhood of the library on Hall Square

Start Point: At the roundabout near the Hand inn car park

DENBIGH WALK

1. From the roundabout, keep the Hand Inn on your right and walk uphill towards Morrisons. In 20m, turn left up Glas Meadows Lane, which narrows to a tarmacked path. Reaching the road, cross diagonally right to continue down Ystrad Llewellyn, and where this bends left, take a footpath between houses on the right.

2. Entering a field, keep along the left side, and in the next field, bear diagonally right towards a white house (Galch Hill). Reaching a stile, cross the track to a kissing gate a little further up, then turn right and climb with the hedge on your right through this and the next field. In a third field bear slightly left on a track continuing into the fourth field.

3. The track emerges at a track junction in front of Gwaenynog. *Hidden from view, the gardens contain a ceramic sculpture of Beatrix Potter. Visits are possible on certain days in summertime only (ask at Denbigh Library).* Keep ahead to pass behind the house, then bend left to go through three gates/stiles and cut across a long field corner. Now bear away from the house on a track descending to the woodland edge, eventually turning right through a  gateway. Beyond this, go left alongside the wood to a stile in its corner, and descend through the trees to a stream and plank bridge.

4. Your onward route is over the stream, but first turn right uphill and walk through the woods for a few minutes to reach the riverside meadow where the Johnson monument stands. *Dr Johnson apparently wasn't too impressed by the urn on the monument. Did his benefactor want to bury him here? But no wonder this was his favourite spot!* Return to point 4, and now cross the stream into the meadow. Walk across it to the gate, after which Dr Johnson's ruined cottage is on the left. Continue up the woodland track (crossing two stiles) to reach a road in about half a mile (1km).

5. Turn right and descend to the hamlet of Lawnt. At the bottom of the hill, turn left into a driveway and immediately left over a stile into a riverside field. Pass the cottage that was once a fulling mill, and continue into the next field where an arched bridge crosses to a picnic area. Keep ahead over a stile, entering woodland. Fork left (uphill) and continue, eventually passing King's Mill and climbing to a road.

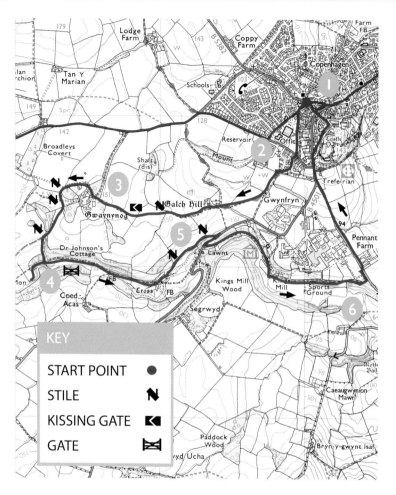

KEY

START POINT	●
STILE	ᴎ
KISSING GATE	◧
GATE	⬚

The buildings high on your left were those of the North Wales Hospital for the mentally ill. It closed in 1995 and is now derelict.

6. Go left on the road for half a mile (1km). Where the castle is signposted, go right, keeping right to reach the castle entrance. *The plaque showing Stanley's birthplace is here.* Bear left past St Hilary's tower and descend Castle Hill through Burgess Gate. Turn right to emerge on the road with the library and Stanley statue on your right. To get back to the roundabout at Lenten Pool, return up the main street and cross the pedestrian crossing to descend an alley (Lon Rosemary). Through the first car park, the roundabout is on your left.

MOEL FAMAU

Feeling on top of the world on Moel Famau

Moel Famau translates as either the 'Mother Mountain' or the 'Mother of Mountains' – but despite that grand title, sadly purists would not consider Moel Famau to be a mountain at all.

There is an official UK government definition that declares a mountain must have a summit above 2,000 feet (610m), and poor Moel Famau can stretch only to 1,818 feet (554m). But it looks like a mountain, it feels like a mountain and, most importantly, it is the highest point of the Clwydian Range.

Moel Famau is easily recognisable from a distance by the bump on its summit – not a natural bump, but the remains of a Jubilee Tower that was erected to celebrate the Golden Jubilee of George III in 1810. A three-tiered Egyptian obelisk was the original design for this, but funds ran out before such a grand structure could be completed, and the memorial

endured this unfinished state until high winds brought it down in the winter of 1862. Just a rather ugly grey stump remains, but it does make the mountain easily distinguishable, and those grey walls now bear a toposcope identifying all that can be seen from this lofty point. So choose a clear day for your ascent and you could well pick out Snowdon, Cadair Idris, Liverpool, the Lake District and more.

There are many paths up Moel Famau, but the route chosen here is a fairly easy and very attractive ascent through the forest to the high moorland. Since the higher part of the forest has now been felled, you will still get good views on the way up. And the descent is on a hard-surfaced track that forms part of the Offa's Dyke Path National Trail. You may well see walkers with their backpacks heading for Chepstow, some 160 miles (250km) away. Will you be tempted to follow them one day?

FOR THE CHILDREN

- Climbing a mountain is a challenge children love. Make sure you take a photograph at the summit for the family album – maybe it will pave the way for future mountaineering exploits.
- Take along a picnic, or at least something with which to celebrate at the summit. And perhaps leave more food in the car to enjoy at one of Forest Car Park's many picnic tables when you return.
- Even children can enjoy the view and they have sharp eyes. Can they possibly pick out Blackpool Tower?
- Take one of the leaflets on offer and you will see that there are many well-marked trails in the Country Park centred on Moel Famau. Finding the ten animals on the short Animal Puzzle Trail (starting from Forest Car Park) is great fun.
- Tell the children about the Offa's Dyke Path. It's 177 miles (285km) long, and walking that – or even part of it – would be a challenge.

And for this walk's Challenge, look out for the acorn symbol of the Offa's Dyke Path, the number 4 in a disc, a wood carving of a black grouse, the number 2961 (search all around the summit), a wooden toadstool, a picture of a dragonfly. Did you see them all? Well done!

THE BASICS

Distance: 4 miles (6.5km)

Gradient: A sustained but never too demanding climb. A waymarked alternative is on offer to avoid the steepest sections

Severity: Moderate/challenging with easier options

Time: 3 to 4 hours

Stiles: None

Map: OS Explorer 265 Clwydian Range

Path description: Well-marked paths traversing woods and moorland

Parking: Forest Car Park on minor road from Llanbedr-Dyffryn-Clwyd to Bryn Eithen (signed from A494). Grid Ref SJ 172611

Toilets: At the car park

Dogs: Dog-friendly but will need leads if sheep are grazing

Refreshment: None on the walk. But there are picnic tables at the car park, so take your own along. And there's the Druid Inn, 2 miles (3km) away at Llanferres

Start Point: From the car park

MOEL FAMAU WALK

1. In the car park, near the boxes dispensing information leaflets, is a post bearing multicoloured arrows, among them the dark blue/purple one you will be following to the summit. Walk uphill in the direction indicated for about 10 minutes to reach a four-way junction. The path ahead is fairly steep, so you are offered the option of a loop to the left  (arrow with white dot). You may not think this worthwhile as the steep section is short and the routes are soon reunited at the next junction. Follow the blue arrow again, climbing through attractive conifer plantations for over half a mile (1km) to reach a clearly marked junction with the track rising steeply ahead.

2. A sign board suggests you may find the path to the left more pleasant, if longer. As you can see the track ahead, you can make an informed choice! But they are telling no lies here – the path left is very much easier, and if you take it you will have views of 'the other side of the mountain' before bending back to wind up to the summit. A kissing gate admits  you to the main track for the last few yards of the ascent.

3. When you have had a look around and identified all the distant landmarks, follow the direction of the Offa's Dyke Path to the south to descend (if you took the last easy loop, it's the path you arrived on). This broad track descends quite steeply initially, and there are views to the left of Foel Fenlli with the Iron Age hill fort on its summit. Later the path takes things much more gently as it winds on for almost 2 miles (3km) to reach the car park at Bwlch Penbarra.

4. Don't miss the toposcope on the right defining the peaks of Snowdonia! Then turn left across the car park to pass through a gate with a green arrow on to a pleasant path running parallel to the road. At one point passing signs for an intriguing 'Numeracy Trail', in just half a mile (1km) it delivers you to the Forest Car Park from which you set out.

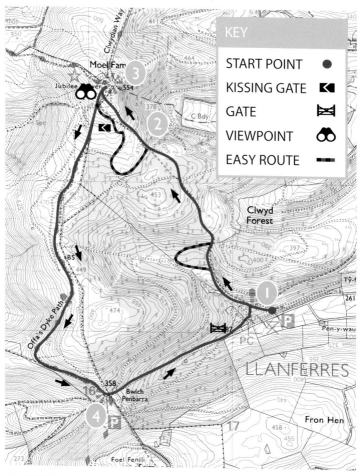

KEY

START POINT	●
KISSING GATE	◤◢
GATE	⋈
VIEWPOINT	👓
EASY ROUTE	▬▬

WEPRE

Wandering through Wepre

You wouldn't have thought of heading for industrial Connah's Quay for a good country ramble? Perhaps not – but then you would be missing something.

At the south of the town the lively little Wepre Brook tumbles through a valley of ancient woodland that abounds with wildlife. And within those woods are the ruins of Ewloe Castle, the surviving gardens of an old manor house, a waterfall, an old bridge, and even a ghost! The whole area is now owned by Flintshire County Council, who have installed a Visitor Centre and children's playground at the northernmost end. Wepre Park is a real gem, and this walk meanders through many of its most fascinating corners before setting out to return along the trackbed of an old railway. But even that's not the end – the path dips back through 'Rosie Woods' and passes a fishermen's pool, finishing the day at the play area. What could be more appropriate?

For the children

- The park is full of interest – bridge, waterfall etc, not to mention the wildlife.
- The ghost here is 'Nora the Nun'. No one is sure how she met her end (she may have drowned in Rosie Pool or been hit by a bomb near the waterfall) but it was somewhere in the park. Keep an eye open for her!
- On a warm day paddling at the ford is popular.
- The playground here is one of the best!

And then there's the Challenge. Can you find an orienteering post bearing the characters 4W, a mosaic, a wood pigeon, a disc bearing the image of a newt, a picture of a badger, a brown dog. Did you spot them all? Brilliant!

THE WALK

1. From the lowest part of the car park take a path going downhill into the valley. Cross the footbridge and continue on the main track (there are several lesser ones here) into the woods. Take the first broad track going uphill on the right, wiggling through the trees to come out at the rim of the valley. Bear left here, and eventually descend steps to cross the bridge in front of the waterfall. *The waterfall was created in the 19th century by the owners of Wepre Old Hall, the manor house that once*

THE BASICS

Distance: 4 miles (6.5km)

Gradient: Gentle climbs only

Severity: Easy

Time : 2½ hours

Stiles: None

Map: OS Explorer 266, Wirral and Chester

Parking: At Wepre Park, Grid Ref SJ 295684 orCH5 4HL

Toilets: At the café

Path description: Well-defined paths in park, roadside pavement, earthen (and sometimes muddy) dismantled railway track

Dogs: Dog-friendly

Refreshment: Café at the Visitor Centre serves all-day breakfasts, snacks, cakes, etc.

Start Point: From the car park CH5 4HL

stood on this site. The water drove a turbine generating domestic electricity.

2. Bear left for a few yards, then turn right up steps. Reaching the wide main track, the former gardens of the Old Hall are directly ahead. *The gardens were landscaped in 1880, and although terribly overgrown today, you can still find a circular pond, a pet cemetery, an arboretum and more. The house itself was once a fine Georgian residence, but fell into disrepair and was demolished in 1960.* To continue the walk, turn left on the main track (right if returning from the gardens) and simply keep ahead (upstream). Soon the gorge narrows and you are walking high above the brook with a bank of red rocks on your right. *The rocks are hard sandstone, very useful as a building material. The Old Hall would have been built of it, as indeed was Ewloe Castle. The red colour comes from oxidation (or rusting) of iron within the rock.* After the rocks continue down steps and along the river to the curious old bridge, Pont Aber. The bridge was removed from upstream and rebuilt on this site around 1800.

3. Do not cross Pont Aber but keep ahead over a footbridge to climb steps leading to Ewloe Castle. *In the 13th century the land here saw many skirmishes between the Welsh and English. Ewloe was built by Prince Llewelyn ap Gruffydd almost as a statement that this territory belonged to Wales. It is a classically 'Welsh Castle', not a fortress built at a vantage point but a solid structure on low ground. The D-shaped keep is typical. Sadly the castle stood for only 20 years before being taken by the English.* Reaching the outer wall, go left to where wooden steps access the castle. Continuing around the periphery, stone steps now lead to a path junction. Bear right then slightly left to a kissing gate beside a wooden gate. Continue across the field beyond to reach the B5125.

4. Turn right on the pavement and continue half a mile (1km) to a fork in the road. Keep left on the main road and walk downhill. At the bottom (250m) turn right down a path passing houses in the valley to emerge at a road. Go left uphill, taking the second road on the right (Bryn Gwyn Lane). Continue for 300m.

5. After the last house on the right go through a kissing gate into Pentre Moch Woods. Here you are on the trackbed of an old railway, and will follow it for the next mile (1.5km). Nearing the end, ignore the footbridge on the right and

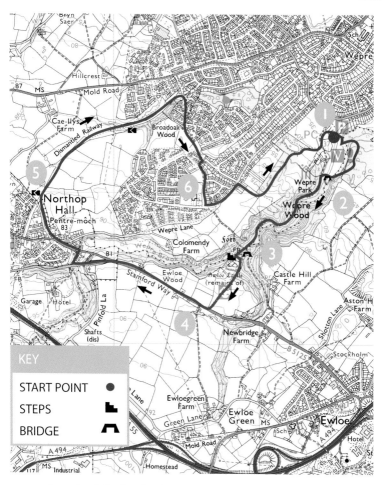

KEY

START POINT ●

STEPS ◣

BRIDGE ⌒

continue ahead, finally going through a kissing gate on to a road in a residential area (Hillsdown Drive). Turn right, uphill, and where the road swings left, take a path behind a metal barrier on the right leading into Llwyni Pond Reserve. Bear left behind the houses, soon crossing a small field and passing another part of the reserve on your left. The path bends right to reach a road.

6. Turn left, pass the school, and continue to a T-junction. Turn left, cross the road, and in 300m take a path between houses on the right entering Wepre Park again. The first path on the left now takes you down through Rosie Woods to Rosie Pool. Once used to stock fish for the Old Hall, Rosie Pool is now popular with local anglers. Bear right to pass the pool, afterwards turning right to return to the Visitor Centre, playground and car park.

NERCWYS FOREST

NERCWYS FOREST AND A LIMESTONE PAVEMENT

THIS IS A WALK IN TWO DECIDEDLY CONTRASTING BUT
EQUALLY FASCINATING PARTS. IT BEGINS WITH A CIRCULAR
TOUR OF LOVELY NERCWYS FOREST, WITH ITS VARIED CONIFER
PLANTATIONS, OLD MINE BUILDINGS AND OUTSTANDING
HILLTOP VIEWS.

The forest was planted in 1965, at a time when the country was thought to be short of
timber after the Second World War. Now this is no longer the case, part of the wood
is being restored to its original state of heathland and bog, while the rest provides
recreational walking, cycling and horse-riding trails.

On leaving the forest you are immediately transported to open limestone hillside where
sheep graze. It's only a gentle climb up Bryn Alyn (1,325ft / 403m), but this is another
world, with limestone boulders, outcrops, and escarpments flanking the path. Your
destination is a rare 'limestone pavement', a flattish area of exposed limestone so
fissured and potholed by millennia of acid rain that from a distance it appears paved. Such
features are scarce outside Britain (where they are generally known as alvar) and are not
that common here either, but they are valuable in that the crevices, or 'grykes', provide
for the growth of unusual plants. In Wales limestone pavements are found only here, on
Great Orme and in the Brecon Beacons. So take a few minutes to study this one – and
then climb just a few feet more to the top of the hill, where the views out to sea, across
to Moel Famau, and down the Alyn valley make a splendid climax to this delightful walk.

FOR THE CHILDREN

> • Forests are always places of enchantment. Think how many fairy tales are
> set in the forest (Red Riding Hood, Babes in the Wood, etc.). Looks out for
> the elves in this one!

- Following the arrows of the 'Circular Trail', the children can lead you round.
- The forest information panels are interesting for children.
- The adults will have to explain about a limestone pavement! The children can have fun balancing their way across it.

And the Challenge? Look out for a pine cone, a holly bush, a picture of a newt, an orange paint dot on a tree, a picture of a bat, a greenhouse. If you got all those you have the eyes of a hawk!

THE BASICS

Distance: 4½ miles (7.25km) (forest circuit only, 2½ miles / 4km)

Gradient: Some gentle inclines

Severity: Easy/moderate

Time: 3 hours

Stiles: 7

Map: OS Explorer 265, Clwydian Range

Path description: Clear forest paths, field paths, grassy tracks

Parking: North entrance to Nercwys Forest on minor road north of Eryrys. Grid Ref SJ 218593

Toilets: None

Dogs: On forest circuit only. Ladder stiles prevent access from forest to Bryn Alyn.

Refreshments: The Sun Inn at Eryrys and the Miners' Arms at Maeshafn are both within a couple of miles

Start Point: From the car park

NERCWYS FOREST WALK

1. From the parking area, go through the gate and up the main track ahead. Take the first track on the left (approx 200m), signed 'Circular Trail'. There are soon good views east towards the Dee estuary, where the trees have been cleared. The obvious track continues around the east side of the forest, crossing a couple of footpaths before arriving at a T-junction with a forest road.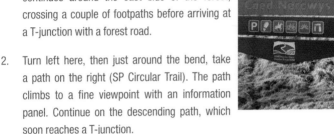

2. Turn left here, then just around the bend, take a path on the right (SP Circular Trail). The path climbs to a fine viewpoint with an information panel. Continue on the descending path, which soon reaches a T-junction.

3. Go left here and continue for about 400m to a path on the left, signed to Llyn Ochin. Taking this path brings you to an area of bog that is being restored. Continue past the information panel and back to the main track. Turn left and keep ahead for a further 400m to a path junction with old mine buildings alongside. *This area was mined for lead between 1851 and 1896. The ruins are those of the office buildings – the mine-head was nearby.*

4. *To get directly back to the car park, keep ahead here, and at the next fork bear right (SP Circular Trail). Reaching the main central track, turn left to return.* For the main route, turn left at this junction, and in 20m, go left again on a path between the pines. Reaching the forest edge, cross the stile to bear half-left across the field, with a large pond below on your right. Cross a ladder stile, and then continue uphill to another. Now keep down the left-hand edge of two fields, cross the top of a narrow third field (farm on your right), and walk down the lane to the road.

5. Turn left on the road and immediately go right up a broad track signed to Bryn Alyn. Keep ahead on this for almost half a mile (1km) to where the track curves sharply right to descend a gully flanked by limestone cliffs. Leave it here and go straight ahead for 100m or so to reach the limestone pavement. When you have taken it in, climb to the top of the hill for the view!

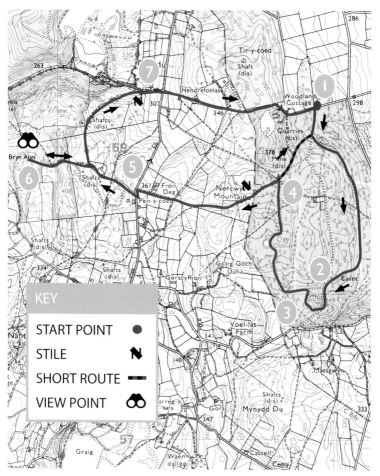

KEY

START POINT	●
STILE	ᴎ
SHORT ROUTE	▬▬
VIEW POINT	👓

6. Now return the way you came as far as a wooden gate post, with a flat plateau of grassland on the left (300m approx). Go half-left across that plateau to go through a gap in a stone wall and a stile in the fence. Descend the field in the direction of the farm to reach a stile in the bottom wall, leading on to the road.

7. Turn right, and at the crossroads, go straight over. Continue up this lane for ¾ mile (1.25km) to reach the car park.

LOGGERHEADS

Along the Leete at Loggerheads

LOGGERHEADS COUNTRY PARK WAS DEVELOPED IN AN AREA THAT WAS ONCE DEVOTED TO LEAD MINING, AND ITS INTRIGUING NAME DERIVES FROM A LONG-STANDING DISPUTE BETWEEN RIVAL MINE-OWNERS.

The Grosvenor family of Llanferres and the Lords of Mold finally resolved their differences in 1763 and erected a boundary stone that is still in place today. Interestingly, the first developers of this site were the Crosville bus company, who from the 1920s onwards would ferry charabancs full of visitors from Liverpool every weekend. A tearoom, a bandstand, a putting green and more were installed to entertain them.

Today's Country Park is centred on a deep gorge cut by the River Alyn through the mineral-rich limestone. The Alyn was always used to power watermills, but because of its limestone bedrock, the poor flow in summertime would often disappear down swallowholes. To overcome this problem, a three-mile-long (5km) leete (or leat) was constructed, drawing water from the Alyn all year round to power pumps draining the lead mines. The first stretch of this walk follows both the Alyn and this leete through a deep gorge with caves, and later vaults the 'Devil's Gorge' on a high footbridge. It's all very dramatic!

Once the gorges have been left behind you have the option of visiting the little village of Cilcain for some resuscitation in its characterful pub before returning across farmland at the foot of Ffrith Mountain. And when you arrive back at Loggerheads again, you can look forward to exploring a restored watermill, discovering local wildlife and history on interactive screens, and tucking into some well-earned refreshment at Caffi Florence.

For the children

- The gorge, caves and Devil's Gorge are all very exciting.
- A pause at Cilcain could fuel the return.
- The 'Room with a View' (interactive exhibits) beside the watermill has lots of interest. And there's the café. . .
- Short legs might prefer just the Cliff Top Circuit – 1½ miles (2.5km) in total.

And for the Challenge, can you spot a wood carving of an owl (look up – sharp eyes needed!), a picture of a dormouse, a squirrel, a lifebuoy, a picture of a church steeple, eggs for sale? Take a bonus if you also see a pig! Well done!

THE BASICS

Distance: 5½ miles (9km) (Cliff Top option adds half a mile (1km))

Gradient: A couple of short sharp climbs

Severity: Moderate. Cliff Top option is the more challenging

Time: 3 hours

Stiles: 8

Map: OS Explorer 265, Clwydian Range

Path description: Easy path through gorge, thereafter field paths and minor roads

Parking: At Loggerheads Country Park Grid Ref SJ 200628 or CH7 5LH

Toilets: At the visitor centre

Dogs: Country Park is dog-friendly. Stiles after Point 4 are prohibitive

Refreshment: Caffi Florence at Country Park open every day for lunches, teas etc. The White Horse at Cilcain en route

Start Point: From the car park

LOGGERHEADS WALK

1. From the car park, leave the Visitor Centre on your right and take the broad path past old trucks loaded with limestone towards the Alyn. The path shortly bends round beside an old waterwheel pit to cross the river. On the far side, turn left and walk downstream to a track junction with a signpost.

2. Keep ahead here following the sign to Devil's Gorge (you can go up the log steps later if you have energy!). The woodland path eventually reaches a kissing gate beside boarding kennels. Continue to the road, cross it directly, and take the path beside the leete channel. *Soon you pass caves that were once mine entrances.* Continue along the leete path, ignoring all side paths, and at a fork, keep left. A bridge carries you across Devil's Gorge, a deep cleft in the rock high above the river. After the gorge the path seems narrower and in places has been provided with railings on the cliff edge. Eventually it emerges at a road.

3. Turn left, going downhill to cross the Alyn. Climb steeply on the far side for about 200m, then at a bend, keep ahead on a signed path beside garden fences. A stile admits you to a field, after which the path hugs the left-hand boundary of several fields separated by handsome stiles. On entering Pentre Millenium Wood (Coed-y-Felin), turn right to reach a seat and sculpture at the top of the hill. Bear left and walk beside the boundary of the wood to arrive at a kissing gate and a road.

4. *The White Horse at Cilcain is about 300m to your right here, and could warrant a diversion.* To continue with the walk, turn left and descend to cross the brook in the hamlet of Pentre, thereafter climbing to a road junction. Cross to a track beside the cottage opposite, and in 50m, bear left through a gate into a field. The path is well signed, maintaining its direction along the right-hand side of two fields, crossing a field in front of a farm and then along the right-hand side of three more fields to reach a cross path near Crug Farm. Keep the same direction, crossing another stile then climbing to the right of trees to reach a stile into woodland on the bank ahead. Wind up the bank to join a broad track.

5. Turn left here and continue past a farm to a road. Turn left and walk down to a T-junction. Cross to a footpath opposite, descending steeply to the Alyn again. Cross on a footbridge and climb to a junction with the leete path. Turn right, and retrace your steps past the kennels to the junction at Point 2. *Now you have a choice. You can simply return the way you came to the Visitor Centre (perhaps staying on this side of the river*

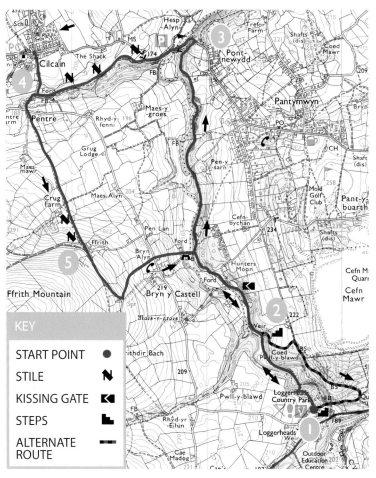

this time) or, for a more energetic option, climb the long flight of log steps on your left to reach the cliff top. If you take the latter, simply keep to the main broad path and you will pass a couple of good viewpoints. On the descent you could opt to go down to the road to see the boundary stone before tackling the steep steps down to the Visitor Centre.

CLYWEDOG RIVER

BESIDE THE CLYWEDOG WITH LADY BAGOT

BORN ON THE HEIGHTS OF CLOCAENOG, THE LOVELY LITTLE
RIVER CLYWEDOG MAKES ITS WAY THROUGH SOME REMOTE
COUNTRYSIDE BEFORE EMPTYING ITS CLEAR WATERS INTO
THOSE OF THE CLWYD NEAR DENBIGH.

In its later days, near the village of Rhewl, the river scurries and tumbles through two miles (3km) of deep wooded gorge cut into the limestone – and all the way it is accompanied by a narrow hard-surfaced track known as Lady Bagot's Drive. Who was Lady Bagot? Well, it's a long story...

Way back in time, all this land was one of five hunting forests belonging to Ruthin Castle. Becoming the estate of Pool Park, and initially belonging to the Salesbury family, it passed by marriage to the Bagots, who in the 1800s rebuilt the original house and landscaped the grounds. The track through this gorge was formerly a rail line used for transporting felled timber from Clocaenog Forest. It was resurfaced for Lady Bagot as a leisure drive, and apparently she particularly enjoyed going this way to church in Llanfwrog on a Sunday morning.

All the Bagot fortunes were catastrophically lost in one bet on the horses in 1928. The lands were divided and the house was used as a rehabilitation hospital, an asylum and more before falling into disrepair. All that remains of their empire is this Lady Bagot's Drive, a lovely woodland walk beside the river, at its best in springtime when wood anemones, primroses and bluebells crowd the path. And of course it is just perfect for an easy family walk. Those with pushchairs or dogs to take into account need do no more than follow the track to its end on the Bontuchel road and return, while those who can climb woodland paths and cross stiles can return across fields at the top of the gorge, with the most splendid views of the Clwydians standing in line across the valley.

FOR THE CHILDREN

- Lady Bagot's Drive is easy walking, and quite passable for the rugged pushchairs of today.
- Woods are always full of interest. Collect pine cones or different leaves, and look out for squirrels.
- The Drovers Arms at the end can be a real carrot when legs are tired!

What about the Challenge for this walk? Can you spot a weeping willow tree, a lime kiln, a round window (sharp eyes needed!), some log steps (i.e. steps edged with big logs), a water trough, and a pond? Claim a bonus prize if you can also spy a black-faced sheep!

THE BASICS

Distance: 4 miles (6.5km). The 'short cut' at Point 4 shortens the route by ¼ mile (0.5km)

Gradient: Moderate incline after leaving Lady Bagot's Drive

Severity: Easy

Time: 2½ hours

Stiles: 8

Map: OS Explorer 264, Vale of Clwyd

Path description: Hard-surfaced track, woodland and field paths

Parking: Grid Ref SJ 109604 or LL15 2UD). Roadside parking near Drovers Arms

Toilets: The Drovers Arms

Dogs: Dogs can run freely on Lady Bagot's Drive. The open fields near the end are grazed by sheep Dogs should take the short cut at Point 4

Refreshments: The Drovers Arms at Rhewl

Start point: The Drovers Arms

CLYWEDOG RIVER WALK

1. From the Drovers Arms cross the A525 diagonally right, following the fingerpost to Bontuchel. Cross the stone bridge over the Clywedog then bear left on a road that soon becomes a rough track. Pass a former mill, then a house,  and cross over the millstream carrying water siphoned from a weir upstream. Continue past lime kilns to reach the house called Tyn-y-Coed, linked by a footbridge to another house (a restored mill) on the opposite side of the river.

2. Keep straight ahead on Lady Bagot's Drive for almost a mile to a path junction near a second footbridge. Again keep ahead (do not cross the river) and climb gently to reach a three-way fingerpost.

3. *The path ahead reaches the Bontuchel road in 150m.* At the fingerpost, turn right on a path climbing determinedly through the trees to a stile. Take the obvious path across the open field beyond (often grazed by cattle) to re-enter the wood via another stile. Continue through the wood until, with a field on the left, a path junction is reached.

4. *The path on the right is a short cut to Point 5 with dog friendly stiles on the way, but you will need leads through the sheep field at Berth. If you take the short cut you will miss the views!* The main route keeps straight ahead here, passing between the trees for another 300 yards before a stile allows exit to an open field. *The Clwydians are before your gaze. Ahead right is the highest of them, Moel Famau (1,818ft / 554m), easily recognisable by the 'bump' of the ruined Jubilee Tower on its summit.* Continue across five fields in succession, all the while maintaining your same direction. In the last field, pass a corrugated barn

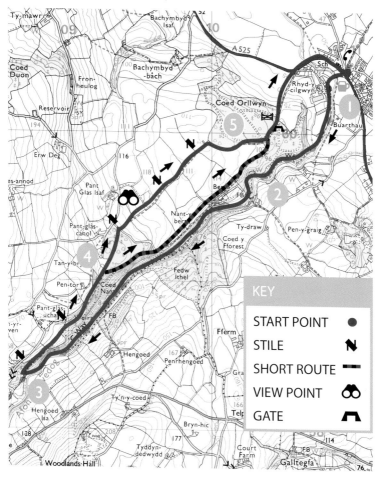

KEY

START POINT	●
STILE	**N**
SHORT ROUTE	▬
VIEW POINT	👓
GATE	∩

and bear right along the side of a wood. At the woodland corner go through a metal gate and continue a few paces to the junction with a track coming from behind right.

5. Bear left and continue downhill to the main road. Turn right, cross the bridge (with care) and return along the verge to the Drovers Arms.

LLYN BRENIG

A Waterside Walk at Llyn Brenig

A large reservoir hidden in forest high on the Denbigh moors, Llyn Brenig was completed in 1976 to help control the flow in the River Dee, and so preserve the water supply to north-east Wales and Liverpool.

It isn't a particularly useful reservoir, taking some four years to fill, and so is only called into service in times of drought. But Llyn Brenig has found another vocation – hiking, biking, horse-riding, fishing and sailing are all practised on or around its shores. In recent years a Visitor Centre has been installed, where you can pick up lots of information on the local wildlife, as well as on the prehistoric remains that have been found on the northern side of the lake.

Of the various hiking trails that have been marked out, the one that completely encircles the lake is surely the best, but at 9½ miles (15km) long, it is sadly outside the scope of this book. The route here gives you just a taste of that perimeter path, setting out from the Visitor Centre to explore the circular Nature Trail, a couple of miles up the shore. It is a pleasant and very easy walk all the way, with some glorious views across the water, and the path beside the stream on the Nature Trail is pure magic. The bonus on the return is the wealth of child-friendly exhibits in the Visitor Centre, a first-class children's playground – and, of course, the excellent cafeteria!

For the children

- Picnic tables are set at intervals along the route, so it might be a good idea to take a few snacks along to keep everyone going.
- Children will enjoy the secret path beside the stream deep in the woods on the Nature Trail.
- The Visitor Centre is full of interest. And thoughts of the refreshment on offer (everything from a full meal to an ice cream) should spur on those tired legs.

And for the Challenge on this walk – can you spot a white boat, a seagull, a blue post, a walking man logo, a fisherman, a wind farm? If you get all six, there could be a reward at the Visitor Centre . . .

THE BASICS

Distance: 6 miles (10km) or 1¼ miles (2km)

Gradient: Very gently undulating along shore

Severity: Easy

Time: 3 to 4 hours

Stiles: None

Map: OS Explorer 264, Vale of Clwyd

Path description: Woodland path beside stream and moorland paths on Nature Trail itself.

Parking: At Llyn Brenig Visitor Centre Grid Ref SH 966547 or LL21 9TT. (For the short walk park near Nature Trail just off A4507 and pick up the route from the crossroads beyond point 2)

Toilets: At Visitor Centre

Dogs: Dog-friendly, but leads may be needed where there are cars

Refreshments: At the Visitor Centre (open every day except Christmas Day)

Start Point: At visitor centre car park

LLYN BRENIG WALK

1. With the Visitor Centre behind you, turn right and walk down the road. In a few minutes you reach the entrance to the sailing club where the road swings left. Continue along it for a further 400m to a road junction. Most traffic takes the exit road to the left here, but you continue ahead, keeping the lake on your right. The road bends in around a creek and then out around a headland, passing several points of access to the shore and picnic tables.  After about 1½ miles (2.5km) a second junction is reached.

2. Keep ahead on the lesser road dipping into the trees. This road has no vehicle access. In about 500m you arrive at a crossroads that feels miles from anywhere. Turn right here and walk down to the old stone bridge, Pont-y-Brenig, at the bottom of the hill. *Pont-y-Brenig looks like a medieval packhorse bridge but probably dates from the 18th century.*

3. Do not cross the bridge but take the narrow path on the right alongside the stream (the Afon Brenig). The path soon crosses a wooden bridge, then follows the twists and turns of this lovely brown stream through grassy clearings deep in the forest, crossing two more bridges on its way. After the last bridge the path enters a Sitka Spruce plantation, dense and quite dark. A ditch is first on your right and then on your left before you cross it and head for a direction post between the trees. Go right, then left (all signed) to climb the bank and leave the plantation near the lake shore (point 4 on the Nature Trail).

4. Turn right on the road, then in 20m, left on a path alongside another plantation, with a deep ditch on your left. At its end the path bears left, crossing the ditch on another handsome wooden bridge. A lesser ditch is now on your left as you make your way across moorland where the trees were recently felled. Reaching a hard-surfaced track (Post 6 here), turn left to quickly return to Pont-y-Brenig. From here you can retrace your steps to return to the car park.

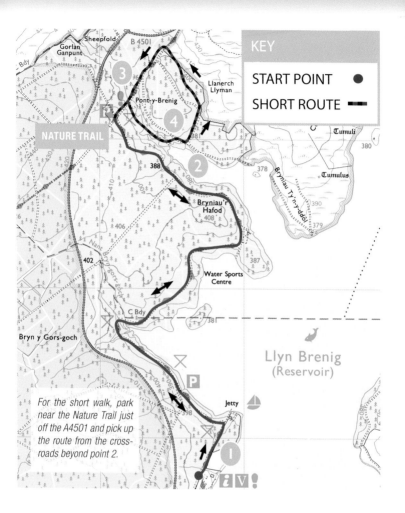

KEY

START POINT ●

SHORT ROUTE ━━━

Sheepfold B 4501
Gorlan
Ganpunt
Llanerch
Llyman
Pont-y-Brenig
NATURE TRAIL
Tumuli
380
388
Bryniau Ty hy-ddol
Cumulus
2
378
390
Bryniau'r
Hafod
408
379
406
387
Nant
402
Water Sports
Centre
C Bdy
381
Bryn y Gors-goch
Llyn Brenig
(Reservoir)
P
*For the short walk, park
near the Nature Trail just
off the A4501 and pick up
the route from the cross-
roads beyond point 2.*
398
Jetty

NANT MILL

Nant Mill and the Lead Mines

The original Nant Mill was probably used for fulling (thickening woollen cloth by beating it underwater with wooden hammers), but from the late 18th century onwards, grinding corn was its only activity.

Falling into disuse in the middle of the 20th century, the mill has now been restored and houses an interesting Visitor Centre with lots of information on local wildlife. The woodland setting is very picturesque and picnic tables are attractively set out on the riverside. This flat area is thought to have once been a 'tenters field', a place where the cloth was stretched out and hung up to dry.

From Nant Mill the first part of the walk follows the well-signed 'Clywedog Trail' upstream beside the rushing river to reach another recently restored industrial site, Minera Lead Mines.

The workforce for these mines came largely from the villages of Coedpoeth and Minera across the valley, and a metalled footpath once used by these miners on their way to and from shifts offers a short cut for the return. The main route, however, continues along the pleasant grassy bed of an old railway line with some good views. Doubling back into the villages, it then meanders through the valley on more old miners' paths to regain Nant Mill. This is a splendid walk packed with interest, and to complete the day there's a playground for the children and the possibility of some well-earned refreshment for everyone at Nant Mill.

For the children

• Nant Mill has a small playground, a piggery with large wooden pigs, 'bird thrones' in the picnic area and a fascinating Visitor Centre.

- At Minera Lead Mines you can visit the reconstructed engine house and see the wheel at the shaft-head.
- Can you imagine the miners clattering along those paths through the valley in their clog-like boots?

Finally, here's your Challenge. Can you spot a greenhouse, a flag, a horse, the initials MCC, the date 1866, a butterfly on a house? Six out of six deserves a reward!

THE BASICS

Distance: 5 miles (8km). Short circuit 3 miles (5km)

Gradient: A couple of sharp climbs out of the valley and corresponding descents

Severity: Moderate

Time: 3 to 3 ½ hours

Stiles: 3, 1 only on short walk

Map: OS Explorer 256, Wrexham and Llangollen

Path description: Grassy and woodland paths, muddy here and there after wet weather. Miners' paths are mostly hard-surfaced

Parking: At Nant Mill Visitor Centre, Grid Ref SJ 289501 or LL11 3BT

Toilets: At Nant Mill, Easter to September

Dogs: Dog-friendly throughout. No impassable stiles or livestock

Refreshment: Nant Mill Visitor Centre offers drinks and snacks (open Easter to September)

Start Point: The Visitor centre at Nant Mill

NANT MILL WALK

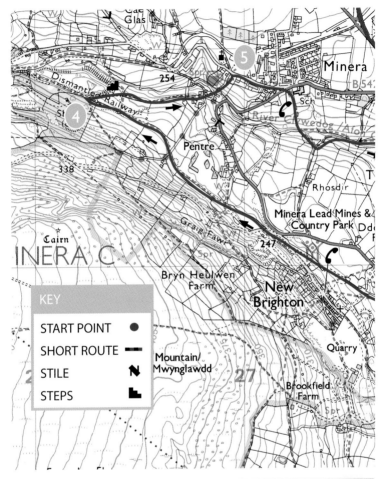

KEY

START POINT   ●
SHORT ROUTE   ▬
STILE   ⋡
STEPS   ◣

1. From the Visitor Centre, take the path closest to the riverside and walk upstream to cross the bridge. Continue up the road until it corners left, then go ahead through a gate into Nant Mill Wood. Continue on the  obvious path until you come down to the riverside at a ford.

2. Keep ahead here and take the uphill path opposite, following the 'Clywedog Trail' signs. The path continues between fences, with the houses of Coedpoeth topping the ridge across the valley. Eventually you reach a stile, after which the path swings left to meet a road.

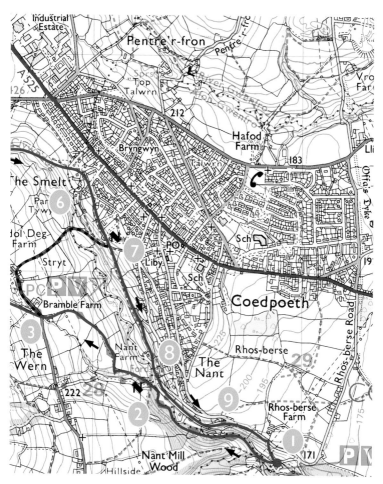

3. *For the short cut, turn right here, then take the first footpath on the right going into the valley. Climb to reach the stile at Point 7.* For the Main Route, cross the road diagonally right to enter the lead mines site. *Evidence shows that there was lead mining here in Roman times. In the Middle Ages it was a profitable business for landowners, although water flooding the shafts was always a problem. By the 19th century engines had been installed to pump out the water, and more than 50 shafts were now dug into the limestone. The ore was removed by rail via*

NANT MILL WALK

the nearby limeworks. Continue up the broad track, passing the Visitor Centre and **Meadow Shaft**. *Meadow Shaft was closed in 1914, when mining was no longer profitable. If you have time, call in at the Visitor Centre for more information.* At the path junction, take the centre path, between the trees, to reach a minor road. Cross this to the path opposite, and shortly cross another road to continue on the broad railway trackbed. In about 600m cross a lane, and after a further 400m pass through a gate on to a hard-surfaced track. Just beyond this the path widens briefly.

4. Turn right here and follow this lesser path through wood and field to emerge on a tarmacked lane. Continue for some 30m, then turn left by a seat on a downhill path. Cross a footbridge over the river, afterwards climbing the steps on the far side to reach a road in Minera.

5. Turn right and descend to the road junction. Cross over to take a path beside the school, dipping into the valley again. Cross the river, then rise to meet a broad track. Turn left here, dropping down to cross the river on a high-sided bridleway bridge. Bear right, then where the path corners left (30m), take a narrow path going into a rough field on the right. After 100m bear left up the bank on a path through the bushes, eventually emerging on a tarmacked lane.

6. Cross to a footpath alongside a yard. At its end walk down the close and turn right. In 60m go left at the T-junction, then take the path on the right beyond the white house. It passes between high hedges before opening up with views of the valley.

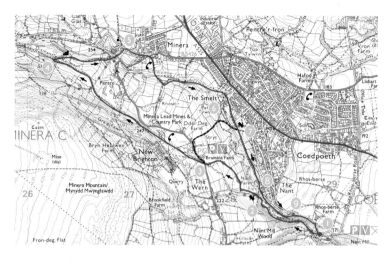

7. On reaching a path T-junction, cross the stile ahead. This path now runs along a field edge, then enters the woods. Follow it down to a road beside a house with stables.

8. Turn left on the road, and continuing left of the ford you met earlier, keep straight ahead to pass the houses. The road climbs gently to reach the 'main' road from Coedpoeth to the mill.

9. Keep ahead (right) here, going gradually downhill until you see a large shed on top of the bank on the left. About 30m after this a path on the right leads down through the trees to return you to Nant Mill.

HOLT

Skirmishes and Strawberries at Holt

Holt is an important frontier town – or at least it was once upon a time! Partly encircled by the River Dee that here forms the boundary between England and Wales, it looks across a handsome sandstone bridge to Farndon.

And when that bridge was built back in the 14th century, it was endowed with the drawbridge and fortified gateway necessary to protect this important crossing into Wales. Frontiers see plenty of conflicts, and in November 1643, Parliamentarian forces under William Brereton attempted to invade Royalist North Wales by crossing Holt Bridge. Fighting lasted two days, with the churches in each village becoming rival headquarters. Eventually the Parliamentarians succeeded, going on to take Wrexham and beyond, but the churches had been damaged and each bears its scars to this day. When you set out, have a look at Holt's north door, where there are three plugged 'loopholes' for those inside to fire through; and if you want more, see the musket ball holes on the west wall inside.

Happily riverside life is more peaceful now and you can enjoy a long stretch of it at the beginning of this short walk. Further along there's the site of a Roman tile factory, an old castle, a medieval market cross, and the Dodgers Barracks on the Strawberry Fields – quite a lot for a small village. Dodgers? Strawberry Fields? Well, wait and see . . .

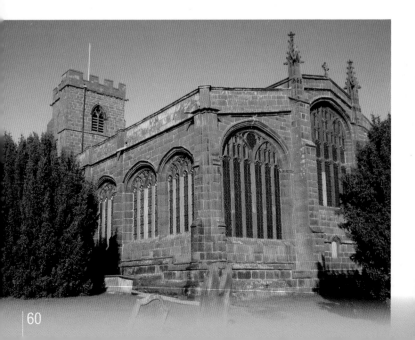

FOR THE CHILDREN

- Children will enjoy finding the evidence of Civil War fighting in the church.
- Bellis's could provide a welcome mid-walk break. And 'Pick your own' in summertime is still popular here – perhaps you could return.
- Unfortunately there's not much of Holt Castle left. Use imagination!

And this time's Challenge? Keep your eyes peeled for a metal water trough, a well (look up!), the date 1870, a picture of three ladies with strawberry baskets, a flagpole, a magpie. Get them all? Brilliant!

THE BASICS

Distance: 3 miles (5km)

Gradient: A virtually level walk

Severity: Easy

Time: 2 hours

Stiles: None

Map: OS Explorer 257, Crewe and Nantwich

Path description: Field paths, quiet lanes. Chester Lane can be muddy in wet weather

Parking: Cross Street Car Park in Holt Grid Ref SJ 410541or LL13 9YG

Toilets: At the car park

Dogs: Dog-friendly, but sheep may be grazing on riverside

Refreshment: Along with Bellis's, there are also pubs and a tea room in Holt

Start Point: From the car park

HOLT WALK

1. At the exit from the car park go left, and then immediately turn right to pass the playground. Ahead of you is the 'Peal of Bells' pub, and beside it the gateway to St.Chad's Church. *Go in and walk down the left side to find the north door. In the churchyard on the opposite side is a column dating from Roman times, now used as a sundial.* Leaving the church, turn right down Bridge Street. Before the bridge, bear right past the hairdressers to a little car park beside the bridge. *The third arch along was the site of the fortified gateway and drawbridge – you can see its extra strengthening.*

2. Go through the kissing gate under the bridge to reach the riverside path. *Wooden chalets, built between the wars, are still in place on both banks.* Continue walking downstream for about 15 minutes until you come to a gate leading on to an earthen lane (Chester Lane).

3. Turn right here, and in about 30m go through a kissing gate on the left. The route now doubles back through fields, which are generally drier underfoot than the lane itself. *These fields were actually the site of a Roman tile factory, supplying tiles and bricks for the fort at Chester.* Emerging on the lane again at the top of the hill, continue ahead to the main road.

4. Turn left on the road and, after about 40m, go right on a track. *On your right now are the one-time Strawberry Fields. In the late 19th century it was found that Holt's soil was particularly favourable for strawberry-growing and many villagers took up the enterprise. For Bellis' it became a big business, with so many strawberries to be picked that a huge workforce was needed in summertime. Coming from far and wide, these pickers were known as Dodgers, and special barracks were built to accommodate them. At the end of the track, the now-dilapidated barracks are on the left-hand side.* Beside the information panel, turn right on to the broad track, and then at the cross-tracks, go left to the main road.

5. Turn left on the main road and pass the main entrance to Bellis's. *A farm shop, a garden centre and a tea room/restaurant are here. It may be worth a pause!* Continue down the Wrexham Road to take the second road on the right.

6. After 100m cross another road and continue downhill on narrow Dee Lane. Just before the overpass, turn left through a kissing gate into a riverside field.

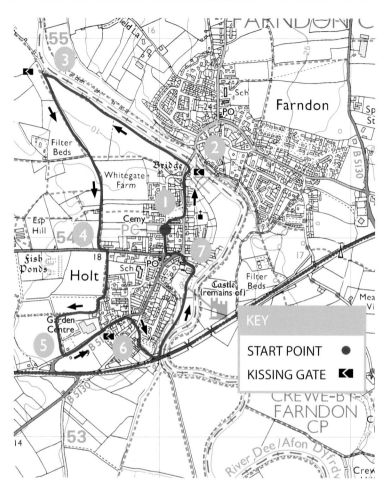

The path soon brings you to the sandstone castle ruins, now well overgrown with ivy. *The castle here was once a fine five-sided edifice, built at the time when Edward 1 was battling with the Welsh on the border lands. The King granted this territory (then known as 'Bromfield') to Earl John de Warenne, who built Holt Castle at the site of an important ford on the Dee. In the Civil War, the castle became a Royalist stronghold.*

7. Past the display board a path leads uphill and emerges on a lane beside the one-time Endowed School. Turning left at the end of this lane you arrive at the medieval market cross in the centre of the village. The car park is down Cross Street on your right.

CORWEN

Hill and Vale around Corwen

The interesting town of Corwen is particularly renowned for its connections with Owain Glyndwr. In 1400 the great warrior and academic pronounced himself Prince of Wales from his manor in the nearby fields.

Today a bronze statue of Glyndwr on horseback presides over the town's central square.

From Corwen, this walk takes you climbing through the beautiful woodland of Pen-y-Pigyn, passing an old Druids' Circle and crossing streams and waterfalls to reach a summit viewpoint. The green valley of the River Dee stretches away to the east, and hills close the horizon all around. Descending to the Dee again, you can opt for a diversion along the old railway line to medieval Llangar Church with its splendid 15th-century wall paintings and minstrels' gallery before continuing on a long, pleasant path beside the rushing river. A final climb takes you to the Iron Age hillfort of Caer Drewyn. Curiously it has none of the usual earth ramparts, but rather is surrounded by a huge rectangular dry-stone wall. The hill isn't a high one, only a mere 965 feet (294m), but the splendid panorama at the summit includes most of the ranges of North Wales.

The route described here is very adaptable, and the sections to Llangar Church and Caer Drewyn can easily be omitted. They are too good to be missed altogether, though – just reserve them for another day!

FOR THE CHILDREN

- Rare red squirrels are occasionally seen in Pen-y-Pigyn!
- Life in a hillfort must have been draughty! Imagine it, and seek out the remains of stone huts near the north-east entrance.
- Watch out for the big birds of prey circling over the hillfort.

And for the Challenge – look out for the date 1416, a dragon on a house gable, a red and white barrier, a telephone box, a rabbit, and a jumping fish logo. On the Llangar Church extension, add a picture of a man slipping over, and the name John Collins. Spotting a red squirrel earns a big bonus!

THE BASICS

Distance: 5 miles (8km). Omitting Caer Drewyn, 3 miles (5km). Llangar Church extension three-quarters of a mile (1.25km) each way.

Gradient: Steepish climbs up both Pen-y-Pigyn and Caer Drewyn

Severity: Riverside and Llangar Church easy. Pen-y-Pigyn and Caer Drewyn moderate

Time: 3 hours (Llangar Church extension 1 hour)

Stiles: 3

Map: OS Explorer 255, Llangollen and Berwyn

Path description: Woodland paths, forest tracks, grassy riverside path

Parking: Corwen free car park (not signed). Access from A5 via lane near Off Licence, Grid Ref SJ 082435 or LL21 0BD

Toilets: At nearby pay and display car park

Dogs: Dog-friendly, but sheep possibly grazing on riverside

Refreshments: Various eating houses in Corwen

Start Point: From the car park

CORWEN WALK

1. Return to the A5 and turn right. After passing the Post Office, go left up a lane for about 400m to turn left where signed to Coed Pen-y-Pigyn. At the top, bear right then left between stone walls. Stepping stones across a stream now lead into the woodland.

2. Keep ahead for 100m, then turn right on an ascending path. *The Druids' Stone Circle, in the angle of these two paths, was created for the Eisteddfod in Corwen in 1919.* Continue uphill, climbing steps, passing a seat, and crossing more waterfalls, to reach the viewpoint with its conical monument. *This stone cairn was erected in 1863 to commemorate the marriage of Edward, Prince of Wales (later Edward VII) to Princess Alexandra of Denmark, and restored in 1911. It is said that from this spot Owain Glyndwr flung his dagger, marking a stone some distance below. This dagger-imprinted stone can now be seen on a lintel in the south porch of the church – you might like to check it out on your return.*

3. Take the higher path leaving the monument and climb gently. At a track bear right, and in 40m, right again on a forestry road.

4. After almost half a mile (0.75km) fork right on a track descending past a cottage. Go through a wooden gate and descend on a sunken track to reach a path junction beside another gate. Keep ahead, downhill, to meet a road.

5. Turn right, and, in 100m, left down a long flight of steps to a road junction on the A5 .

6. *Here begins the optional extension to Llangar Church along the old railway track – the path is signed in the angle between the A5 and B4401. The route originally crosses landscaped gardens where you should keep straight ahead to pick up the obvious line of the railway. Just under a mile (1.25km) later, at a white house, turn left, then left through a signed gate to reach the church. Llangar Church is in the care of Cadw, and is open in summertime only.* The main route continues on the A5 across the River Dee (take care), then over a stone stile on the right. Keep to the obvious path flanked with stone slabs beside the river, eventually ducking into a field and returning via a stile into woodland on the right. Cross a footbridge and climb to enter a field. The path hugs its right-hand border, but in the next field bends sharply uphill, going through a gate and then a kissing gate to meet the road.

7. *Turning right here offers a short cut to Point 9.* To continue up Caer Drewyn, cross to the lane opposite and at a fork in half a mile (0.75km), bear right (signposted Caer Drewyn). Turn right and quickly left through a gate to enter the fort area. The broad track climbs steadily, bending around the hill. After it levels at the north-east corner (number 6 on sign), turn left through a gap in the ramparts,

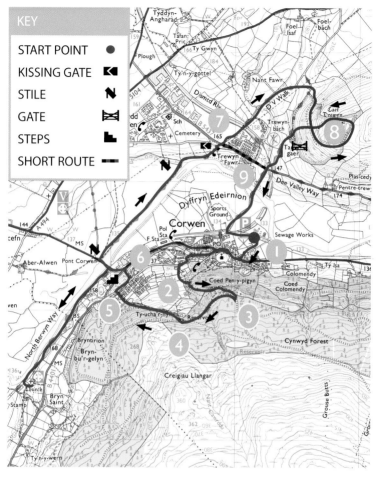

KEY

START POINT ●

KISSING GATE ◄

STILE ◢

GATE ⬔

STEPS ◣

SHORT ROUTE ▬▬

and bear right to reach the summit cairn. *Caer Drewyn hillfort was built about 2,500 years ago. The outer wall enclosed numerous small huts, whose remains you can see near the north-east corner.*

8. To continue, take the clear grassy path descending. After crossing the track on which you came, it reaches the foot of the hill. Go left through a gate and continue to a road. Turn right.

9. Go left over the river bridge. Approaching town, turn up a grassy bank on the left, then along the old railway to return to your car in the car park.

VALLE CRUCIS ABBEY

Valle Crucis Abbey and the Holy Grail

There cannot be a short walk more packed with interest than this one! The centrepiece is Valle Crucis Abbey, a 13th-century Cistercian establishment, ruined, but still displaying a fine west wall with rose window and a lot more.

The abbey was built over an early wooden church and the site is thought by some to be the 'Glastonbury' to which Joseph of Arimathea carried the Holy Grail.

The story goes that that chalice was then buried on the hill known as Castell Dinas Brân (the one with the ruins on top), but no, it isn't there any longer! Just up the road from the abbey, another enigmatic tale relates to Eliseg's Pillar, erected in the 9th century by one Concenn, Prince of Powys, in honour of his great-grandfather Eliseg. The inscription from that time has been worn away, but it has been recorded and it mentions the chieftain Vortigern, known to be implicated in the Merlin saga. Fact and fiction intertwine – could this be the scene of Arthurian legends?

Add to all that the Horse Shoe Falls where the water for the Llangollen Canal is taken from the Dee, and the first stretch of that glorious canal itself, now enjoying World Heritage status. And then there's an old chain bridge over the river, a restored railway

station, a balcony path with superb views up the valley, a section on the National Trust's Velvet Hill and even a couple of refreshment stops en route. What more could you want?

For the children

> • The meadow near the Horse Shoe Falls is great for a picnic, and there are places where children can paddle at the edge of the river to catch tiddlers.
> • The canal water here is very clear. With luck you should be able to spot fish both large and small.
> • Children love King Arthur stories!
> • The promise of an ice cream (or more!) at the Abbey tearoom could work wonders.

And the Challenge this time is to spot a horse, a fish, an old petrol pump, a train (hearing one will do!), the name 'Fungusfut', and a picture of a blue tractor. You got all those? A prize is in order . . .

THE BASICS

Distance: 4½ miles (7.25km)

Gradient: Just a couple of short steepish sections

Severity: Easy/moderate

Time: 2 hours

Stiles: 2

Map: OS Explorer 265, Llangollen and Berwyn, or 256 Wrexham and Llangollen

Path description: Canal towpath, hillside footpaths and field path. Two very short steepish ascents

Parking: Llantysilio Green Car Park Grid Ref SJ 198433 (off A542, SP Rhewl).

Toilets: In the car park

Dogs: Dog-friendly except for the ladder stile in Point 3

Refreshments: The Chain Bridge Hotel and Abbey Farm Tearoom are on the route

Start Point: From the car park

VALLE CRUCIS ABBEY WALK

1. From the car park return to the road and head left. At the church (500m), go through a gate alongside the lych gate and take the path towards the river, emerging in a meadow beside the Horse Shoe Falls. *The falls were designed by Thomas Telford in 1806 as a means of diverting water from the Dee to supply the canal. Unfortunately, so much water was drawn that several mills downriver went out of business.* Go through the gate beside the pumping station and continue on the canal towpath, soon passing the Chain Bridge Hotel, with restored Berwyn Station across the river.

   An entrepreneurial merchant built the original chain bridge around 1800 to allow him to carry slate, coal and limestone between the A5 and the canal without crossing the toll bridge in Llangollen. The current structure was closed when it was declared dangerous around 30 years ago, it is scheduled for restoration. Continue beside the canal. After the first bridge the towpath is no longer tarmacked. At the second bridge leave the canal (just after the Motor Museum), cross the bridge and turn right, going uphill beside the main road.

2. *For a short cut, you can take the path going left in front of a yellow house (SP Valley Crucis Abbey) to reach Point 4.* At the top of the rise, take the minor road going steeply uphill on the left to reach a road junction. Turn left here and, in 100m, go left on a signed track. Beyond the house go through a gate and then through a second gate on to a path with superb views up the Dee Valley, and later of Valle Crucis Abbey. Continue on this gently descending track to a junction at the bottom.

3. Turn sharp left here and soon bear right to a gate with a stile alongside. Over the stile, walk towards the cottage, where there is a ladder stile on the left. Cross this stile and keep to the right side of the field, passing through a gate into a second field.

4. At a signpost, turn down steps on the right and cross the footbridge over the stream. *The pond on your left was originally the monks' fishpond.* Continuing through the caravan site you arrive at the entrance to the abbey. Walk ahead up the road to reach the farm buildings and tearoom.

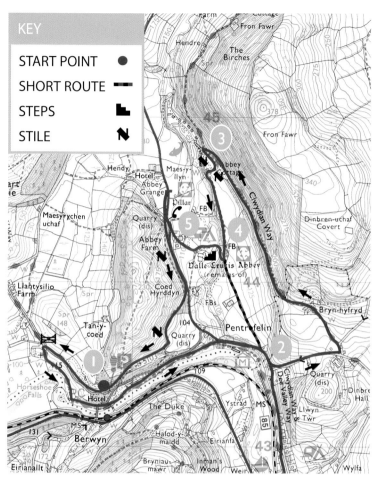

5. Bear right here, and continue on the footpath alongside the A542 for 300m to visit Eliseg's Pillar (on the right). *Fortunately the original inscription on the pillar was written down by historian Edward Lhuyd in 1696. The pillar itself was broken in the Civil War and only the base remains. Excavations in 1773 revealed the skeleton of a tall man buried beneath. Current excavations are being carried out by Bangor and Chester Universities.* Walk back along the road and continue on the raised footpath. Pass the abbey and at a pull-in lay-by, take a signed path over a stile on the right. A brief climb now takes you to a pleasant path around the side of Velvet Hill. Eventually reaching a stile on the left, cross and descend to a road junction. Bear right on the wider road (granite lodge on your right) and walk on a few yards to regain the car park.

LLANGOLLEN

ROCKS AND RUINS AT LLANGOLLEN

THIS IS A TRULY ACTION-PACKED WALK, A REAL CLASSIC NOT TO BE MISSED. THE TOWN OF LLANGOLLEN IS BEST KNOWN FOR ITS INTERNATIONAL MUSICAL EISTEDDFOD, HELD ANNUALLY IN JULY, BUT IT HAS MANY OTHER ATTRACTIONS, INCLUDING EIGHT MILES (13KM) OF SCENIC RAILWAY, AND HORSE-DRAWN BOAT TRIPS ON A PICTURESQUE CANAL.

Looking out over the town are the hilltop ruins of one-time fortress Dinas Brân, and every visitor wants to get up there because they can just tell that the view will be magnificent. And so it is, extending across the Cheshire Plain to the east, up the long winding Dee Valley to the West, and along the length of the impressive limestone escarpment behind. These 'Eglwyseg Rocks' were once a coral reef under a tropical sea and fossils of ammonites and trilobites abound.

This route gives you a taste of everything, setting off from the Eisteddfod Pavilion, climbing to the summit of Dinas Brân, then skirting the Eglwyseg Rocks before returning along the canal. The ascent to Dinas Brân is less severe than you might expect because the path zig-zags widely up the grassy slope. And the prospect from the summit makes it all worthwhile (although there is an alternative for those who would rather not tackle it). Back down at the foot of the Rocks, you can look out for the huge ravens that inhabit these sheer cliffs, and you might turn over a few stones to hunt for a fossil. After all that activity, a pause at the Sun Trevor Inn could be welcome before the gentle return beside the canal. Boats are on the move all year round, and the obvious complexities of navigating this narrow section of waterway ensure there's never a dull moment for those on the towpath.

FOR THE CHILDREN

- A photograph on the summit of Dinas Brân is mandatory!
- There's not much castle left, but make sure you explore the 'secret passageway' (at the back, near the keep and map).
- Look out (and listen) for ravens. They look like big crows, but they make a noise like a cough or croak as they fly overhead.

- Hunt for fossils. The best ones are on the higher part of the scree (difficult to reach) but you can find some on the lower slopes, too.
- Narrowboats are always interesting. Can you see one painted with traditional 'roses and castles'?

And now the Challenge. Can you spot a picture of a knight, the number 41, a yellow salt bin, a boat with a dog on board, and an acorn sign (for the Offa's Dyke Path)? If you get all five, go to the top of the class (and perhaps get an ice cream at the Wharf Café)! Spotting a raven or a fossil should earn a bonus!

THE BASICS

Distance: 5 miles (8km)

Gradient: Sharp climb up Donkey Hill. Dinas Brân itself is less steep

Severity: Moderate/challenging on Dinas Brân. Easier route around base

Time: 3 hours

Stiles: None

Maps: OS Landranger 256, Llangollen and Wrexham

Path description: Grassy and shingly tracks, quiet roads, canal towpath

Parking: Llangollen Eisteddfod Pavilion on A542 (at silver harp). Grid Ref SJ 210425 or LL20 8SW

Toilets: None

Dogs: Dog-friendly but sheep usually grazing on Dinas Brân

Refreshment: The Sun Trevor Inn is mid-walk, Llangollen Wharf has a pleasant café

Start Point: From the car park

LLANGOLLEN WALK

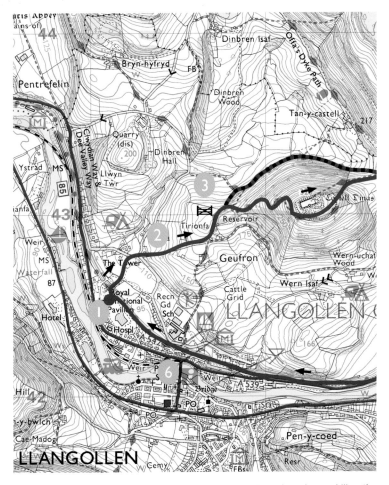

1. From the car park walk up to the canal bridge, cross it, and continue uphill on the tarmacked path. Cross between playing fields to a gate near the pavilion. Turn right on the road to arrive at a four-way junction.

2. Cross over directly to climb Donkey Hill. *The name dates from a century or so ago, when there was a teashop on the top of Dinas Brân, and the necessary supplies were carried up this way by donkey.* At the junction at the top, turn left, uphill, to a gate leading on to Dinas Brân

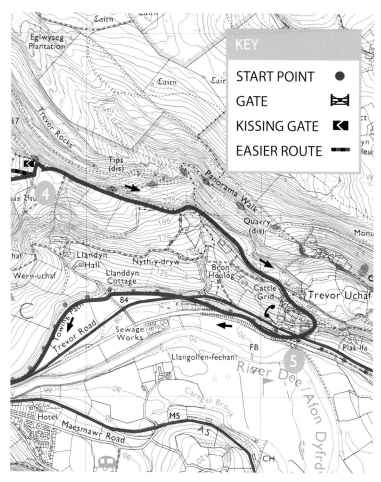

KEY

START POINT	●
GATE	⋈
KISSING GATE	◄
EASIER ROUTE	━━

3. Here the route divides. For the alternative route, omitting the hilltop castle, keep left. Stay beside the fence on your left for about half a mile until you pass through a gate into rough pasture. Keep ahead here, climbing steadily to reach the kissing gate at Point 4. For the main route, keep ahead up the rough-hewn steps. Cross the flat grassy area and go down a brief dip before joining the obvious railed zig-zag path leading to the summit. *An Iron Age hillfort once occupied this summit – you can still see the ramparts. The castle was built around 1260 by one Gruffydd II ap Madog, a marcher lord, and was lived in for a mere 17 years. When Edward I was campaigning against the Welsh in this area, Gruffydd's sons decided to burn*

down the castle themselves rather than let the English take it. Walk straight across the summit, keeping right of the passageway wall to find the descending path. *There are extensive views across the Cheshire Plain here. In the foreground you can see the viaduct vaulting the River Dee near Rhosymedre.* Continue downhill, passing through a gate into sloping pasture. Pass gorse bushes on the right to go through a kissing gate.

4. Turn left towards the base of the Eglwyseg Rocks. Over the cattle grid turn right and continue for approx. 400m with the fossil-rich scree spilling down the slopes beside you. At a road fork keep right, descending past isolated houses and finally curving sharply to reach the Sun Trevor Inn on the A583.

5. Cross the road to go over the canal bridge and turn right to the towpath. Simply

keep ahead (canal on right!) all the way back to Llangollen. *At first there are good views down the valley to Llangollen. In several places the canal is merely one boat wide, and the sharp bend at Bridge 42 can be tricky for longer boats. The final section, cut out from the granite bedrock, is quite dramatic.*

6. Finally reaching Llangollen Wharf, pass the café and stables and continue to the next bridge. This is the one you crossed earlier – leave the canal to return to the car park.

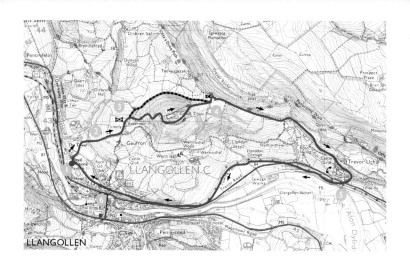

PONTCYSYLLTE AQUEDUCT

Pontcysyllte Aqueduct and Llangollen Canal

Revelling in its new World Heritage status, Telford's impressive aqueduct strides boldly across the Dee Valley on 19 heavy grey pillars. Some 126 feet (38m) below the river rushes and tumbles between wooded banks while tiny dots of sheep graze the fields.

Walking across the aqueduct is an experience not to be missed, and you can take it in either at the beginning or end of this walk, but be warned – this is not one for vertigo-sufferers!

Telford built his aqueduct in 1805, at a time when it was still intended that the canal should travel north to reach the coast near Ellesmere Port. Bizarrely, the company promptly ran out of money, being unable to fund either locking over Ruabon mountain or blasting their way through it. Since the water supply for the whole canal was to come from those heights, another solution was needed urgently. And so it was decided to turn the canal west to Llangollen, where water could be taken from the Dee. This five-mile long (8km) 'feeder canal' is some of the most scenic waterway in Britain, and you get to see just a little of it on this route, which also includes a ramble through beautiful conifer woods, and an open hillside path with splendid views over the Vale of Llangollen. This is a first-class walk, and there's even a friendly pub to resuscitate you near the halfway point!

For the children

- Crossing the aqueduct is an adventure – and you can even pick up a certificate for doing so in the shop at the Anglo-Welsh boat base.
- The Heritage Centre near the aqueduct's end can tell you a lot more about the building of the aqueduct.
- The Offa's Dyke Path. Signed by National Trail Acorns, this runs for 177

miles (285km) down the Welsh borders between Prestatyn and Chepstow. If you meet anyone carrying a rucksack, ask them if they are going all the way. How long will it take them?

• The promise of a drink (or more) at the Sun Inn will spur on any tired legs.

• Boats on the canal are always fascinating. See if you can get a look inside one at the base.

And what about the Challenge? Can you spot a horse, the number 50 in a circle, a pine cone, someone playing golf (look in the distance!), a 'No fishing' sign, a male mallard (brightly coloured duck). If you get all those you have 'Super-vision!'

THE BASICS

Distance: 4 miles (6.5km)

Gradient: Gentle climb through Trevor Woods

Severity: Easy

Time: 2½ hours

Stiles: 4

Map: OS Explorer 256, Wrexham and Llangollen

Path description: Coniferous woodland, hillside path, canal towpath

Parking: Trevor Basin Car Park (free), Grid Ref SJ 271422 or LL20 7TT

Toilets: At The car park

Dogs: Dog-friendly. All stiles can be bypassed

Refreshments: At Trevor Basin; the Anglo-Welsh Boat Hire base and The Telford Inn, The Sun Trevor Inn is approximately at the halfway point

Start Point: The car park

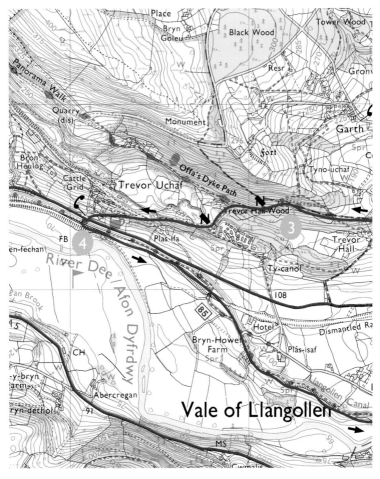

1. Leave the car park by the gate leading to the canalside and turn left. Continue past moored boats, over a small swing bridge, and past the Heritage Centre to the start of the aqueduct. *You really must make time to cross this either now or at the end of the walk.* Whether or not you made the crossing, you now need to take the path between the picnic tables and the start of the aqueduct. It goes down steps, bears right to pass under the arches, then climbs to the road. Turn right on the road, cross the bridge, and take the path immediately left. Continue with the canal on your left (do not cross the iron bridge) to a

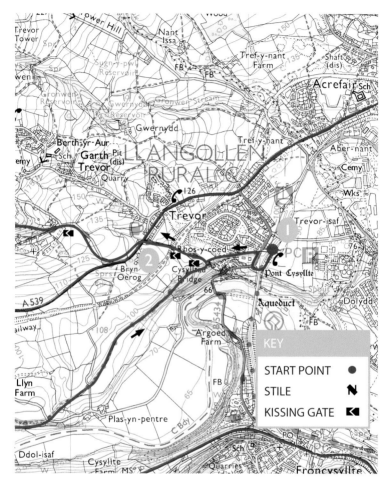

KEY

START POINT	●
STILE	N
KISSING GATE	◄

kissing gate. Here you are joining the Offa's Dyke Path and it bears diagonally right across the field to another kissing gate, then under the disused railway, turning right then left to reach the A538.

2. Cross the road and turn left on the pavement, climbing gently. At the summit,

take the road on the right (SP Offa's Dyke Path) and in 400m, at a right-hand bend, go straight ahead up the drive to Trevor Hall. After 100m pass through a kissing gate on the right, afterwards climbing steeply through woodland. Continue alongside a field, then, at the entrance to Trevor Woods, keep ahead downhill. At the next two track junctions keep left, sticking with the Offa's Dyke Path. Soon a strong path joins from behind right and about 60m further along the track forks.

3. Leave the Offa's Dyke Path here and keep left, downhill. At the bottom, go over a stile, then through more open woodland before bending left up the side of a field. Cross a stile and turn left on the gravelled track to descend. Leave the track at the first left-hand bend to keep straight ahead over a grassy area to a metal gate and stile. Through the gate the grassy track descends steadily (ignore the track to the quarry on the right) and there are splendid views into the valley with Llangollen in the distance. Go over another stile and continue to join a road at a bend. Keep ahead downhill through the hamlet of Sun Bank to reach the A538 again, with the Sun Trevor Inn alongside.

4. Cross the road diagonally right to go over the canal bridge. Turn right to reach the towpath, then go right, passing under the bridge. With the canal on your left, simply keep ahead for two miles (3km) to return to Trevor. *This stretch of canal has been the scene of several severe breaches*

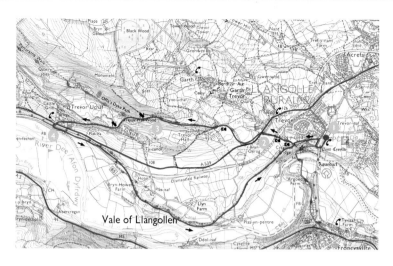

in the past. In the first section, just beyond the Sun Trevor Inn, the railway once ran parallel and below. A terrible breach in September 1945 washed away the whole bank and caused the derailment of the early morning mail train, with the death of the driver. Where the towpath ends, double back over the wrought iron bridge to reach the path you set out on earlier. Retrace your steps to Trevor Basin and the car park.

ERDDIG

Exploring Erddig

THE 18TH-CENTURY HOUSE OF ERDDIG HAS WON MANY ACCOLADES SINCE THE LAST SQUIRE, SIMON YORKE, GAVE IT TO THE NATIONAL TRUST IN 1973.

The Yorke family were serious hoarders and are believed to have saved all of the documents, ledgers, kitchen implements and children's toys they had accumulated over the years. It was Simon Yorke's express wish that, under the care of the National Trust, not an item should leave the house. And that's what makes a visit so fascinating – each room, including the workshop, smithy and stables, looks just as if the inhabitants have popped out for a few minutes. Particularly interesting is the Yorke family's respect for their servants, evidenced in their records and the portraits gracing the walls of the servants' hall.

Given all this, you really will want to make a visit to the house when you come here – but equally appealing is Erddig's attractive parkland with so many fascinating features. The walk here includes the site of a Norman castle, a curious 'cup and saucer' waterfall, the banks of the River Clywedog, and swathes of ancient woodland. At around four miles (6.5km) in length it should not take you more than a couple of hours, but it can easily be adapted to meet your family's requirements.

FOR THE CHILDREN

- The Cup and Saucer. Adults could read the information panel and try to explain how the water gets uphill!
- If the Clywedog is not in spate it may be possible to paddle from the shingly banks.
- Erddig House has lots to interest children, including a special Children's Trail.

And for the Challenge, see if you can spot a blackbird, a drawing of two badgers, a three-legged seat carved from a log, a rider on horse sign, a disc showing a mill with a waterwheel, a black dog. If you got them all, you have eyes like a hawk!

THE BASICS

Distance: 4 miles (6.5km)

Gradient: Only one short gentle climb on road

Severity: Easy

Time: 2 hours

Stiles: None

Map: OS Explorer 256, Wrexham and Llangollen

Path description: Tarmacked paths, well-defined tracks

Parking: Erddig House, Grid Ref SJ 328481 or LL13 0YT. Free car park in orchard

Toilets: Erddig House

Terrain: Tarmacked paths, well-defined woodland tracks

Dogs: On leads where sheep are grazing, free-running in woodland

Nearest food: Restaurant in Erddig House for those going inside, otherwise tea garden in grounds open in summertime. Café after Point 5

Start Point: The Orchard car park

ERDDIG WALK

1. Leave the orchard car park the way you came in and turn right on the access road. At the signposted junction, bear right towards 'Cup and Saucer'. The wide metalled track now descends alongside an iron fence. Keep ahead as far as a footbridge on the left.

2. The footbridge leads to the 'Cup and Saucer', with an explanatory panel nearby. *The circular waterfall was built in 1775 to provide the inflow to a hydraulic ram, pumping water up to the house.* Return over the footbridge and continue down the track to a small iron gate on the right.

3. Go through the gate on an earthen track that doubles back, then bends left to ascend steps. *Here you are on the flank of the 8th-century Wat's Dyke. Some 50 years older than the better known Offa's Dyke, Wat's nevertheless stretched 60 miles (100km) from Welshpool to Holywell.* Between the two flights of steps turn left on to a narrow path along the slope. After passing a seat it soon drops into a gully where

    an information board describes the Motte and Bailey castle. Now climb to reach a level plateau with an avenue of beech trees crossing it. *The defensive structure here took advantage of Wat's Dyke, and was built in the late 11th century. It was probably the 'Castle of Bromfield' referred to in ancient texts. At this point you are standing in the bailey, or courtyard, which would have been surrounded by high fencing. The beech avenue is an 18th-century landscaping addition. If you turn left in the middle of the avenue a track leads down and then up to the highest point, the motte, where a keep would once have stood.* Return the way you came as far as the iron gate and turn right on the metalled track. Cross the stone bridge over Black Brook and keep ahead to a path junction beside a larger bridge over the Clywedog.

4. *Cross the bridge for a short cut to Point 6.* For the main walk, turn left here and continue upstream through the meadow. After a kissing gate, the path crosses a level field with the Clywedog twisting and turning away on the right. Go through another gate and keep ahead to leave the estate beside a brick cottage.

5. Turn right and cross the bridge. *You are now in the hamlet of Felin Puleston and there is a café in the industrial estate on the left should you want a pause.* Now go through a kissing gate on the right. After a few yards branch left into the wood and continue on this path along the foot of Wat's Dyke again. After three-quarters of a mile (1.25km) you reach a tarmacked track.

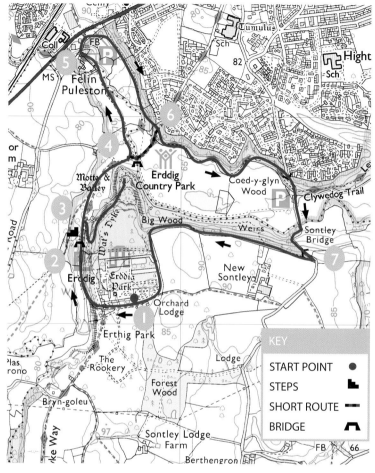

KEY

START POINT ●

STEPS ⌐

SHORT ROUTE ▬

BRIDGE ⌐⌐

6. Cross straight over and continue through the wood for another mile (1.5km) to a car park beside the road. Turn right on the road, cross the river, and climb steeply. After a sharp right-hand bend at the top, go through a kissing gate on the right.

7. Follow the broad path along the edge of the wood, passing a path leading down to the site of a former watermill. *It is possible to go down there, but nothing remains of the mill and the path is somewhat overgrown.* Continue along the main path to the woodland corner. Here bear left and walk alongside the wall. Soon there is a magnificent view of the house, lake and formal gardens, seen through fine wrought iron fencing. Keep ahead to pass the octagonal dovecote and return to the orchard car park.

CHIRK CASTLE

CHIRK CASTLE AND THE CEIRIOG VALLEY

STARK, SOLID, GREY, AND EVERY CHILD'S IDEA OF A FORTRESS, CHIRK CASTLE STANDS GAUNTLY ON ITS HILLTOP CLOSE TO THE ENGLISH BORDER. ALONG WITH SO MANY OTHERS, IT WAS BUILT IN THE LATE 13TH CENTURY, A TIME WHEN EDWARD I WAS SEEKING TO MAINTAIN A MILITARY PRESENCE IN REBELLIOUS WALES.

Most strongholds from this period are now in ruins, but Chirk has survived intact, having been bought by the Myddelton family in 1595, and lived in continuously by them until very recently. Today it is in the care of the National Trust, and visits here include the medieval tower and dungeon and the elegant 17th-century Long Gallery, along with landscaped gardens that merit time in themselves.

With all this to see you won't want a long walk, and this one at 3½ miles (5.5km) allows you to take in something of the castle's parkland along with a short stretch along the lovely River Ceiriog, here forming the boundary between England and Wales. It also visits the site of the 12th-century Battle of Crogen, where a gaunt oak tree is estimated to be more than a thousand years old. The paths across the estate are used by kind permission of the landowner, but you should note that they are only open between 1st April and 30th September each year. So time your visit accordingly to enjoy this gem of a walk on the borders of Wales.

FOR THE CHILDREN

- In Chirk Castle grounds children can try building their own den (wood provided, bring your own covering), while under-5s have an area dedicated to sit-and-ride tractors.
- If you go into the castle, make sure you get the Children's Trail leaflet.

• Think about the age of that oak tree. It was probably a sapling when William the Conqueror landed on these shores.

And for the Challenge, see if you can spot a red hand (other than the one on the castle gates!), a map of ancient Wales, an old bath, a clock with Roman numerals (sharp eyes needed!), a wooden 'Welcome to Shropshire' sign, a disc with a buzzard logo. Did anyone get all those? Excellent!

THE BASICS

Distance: 3½ miles (5.5km)

Gradient: Two very short steep climbs. Otherwise gently undulating

Severity: Easy/moderate

Time: 2 to 2½ hours

Stiles: 5

Map: OS Explorer 240, Oswestry

Parking: Parking for Chirk Castle at Home Farm. Grid Ref SJ 267383 or LL14 5AF

Toilets: In the courtyard at Home Farm

Path description: Field and woodland paths. Short section on quiet lane

Dogs: The whole route is dog-friendly, but dogs will need to be on leads in the castle grounds

Refreshments: Kiosk at Home Farm is open for drinks, ice creams and light snacks on school holidays and fine weekends. Tearoom in the castle itself (paid entry)

Start Point: The car park

CHIRK CASTLE WALK

1. From the car park, return to the access road and turn left. At the junction where a road on the right goes up to the castle, keep straight ahead over a stile and follow the grassy path to the woodland edge (red/white-topped posts). Bear left alongside the wood to pass through a kissing gate, and continue 150m to another kissing gate on the right. Go through and walk across the field, following white-topped posts to a distant fence. Bear left, passing left of a spinney to a kissing gate beside a cottage. Walk down to the road.

2. Turn right, and where the road corners left (200m), keep ahead towards the caravan site. *The splendid wrought iron gates here were constructed by the local firm Davies Brothers around 1720. Above the gates you can see the Myddelton crest with its red 'bloody' hand. One story goes that two young Myddeltons, disputing the ownership of the castle, decided to settle the matter with a race to its gates. It was very close, but as one reached out his hand to touch the gate first, a supporter of the other quickly drew his*  *sword to sever the extended wrist.* Passing the caravan site entrance, continue to a path junction beside a wall. Turn right and descend through woods.

3. At the main road, turn right, then go left to cross the bridge (Pont Faen) over the Ceiriog. You are now in England – the river is the boundary here. Turn right, and in 150m cross a stile to the right of the first cottage to continue through lovely riverside meadows. Reaching a gate and stile, keep straight ahead beside the river. The path now meanders through  woodland, crossing an entrant stream, and climbing a long flight of steps up the bank. Leave the wood via a stile and bear left to go through a kissing gate. Continue up the track, passing cottages, to reach the lane at the top.

4. Turn right here and descend, passing the old schoolhouse and, later, lime kilns. At the road junction at the bottom, turn right and descend steeply to the river bridge at Castle Mill. *A plaque on the bridge commemorates the Battle of Crogen here in 1165. Henry II had mustered an army at Oswestry, thinking to conquer North Wales. On hearing of this, Owain Gwynedd, Prince of Wales, quickly assembled what troops he could to counter the attack. The Welsh were far outnumbered but in this*

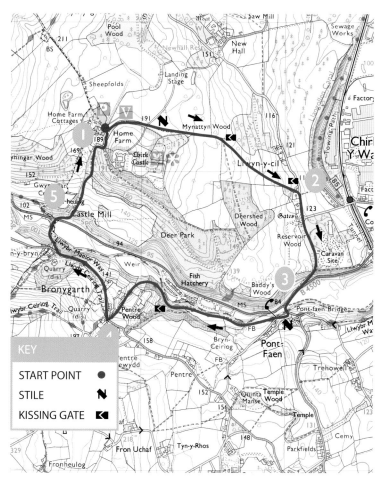

thickly wooded valley they ambushed the king. Henry had his woodsmen cut down all the trees, but by stealth and tactics the Welsh won the day.

5.   Cross the road, bearing right to join a track. *Information panels describe the battle, and beyond stands the 'Oak at the Gate of the Dead', the venerable tree that somehow survived Henry's woodsmen.* Continue up the track and climb the steep bank. Cross a stile to walk up the left side of the field with the bank that is Offa's Dyke on your left. Cross another stile, then follow a short track to a gravelled road. Turn left and climb to a junction with a tarmacked road. The castle is ahead here, and Home Farm, where you started, is just to the left.

PISTYLL RHAEADR

Around Pistyll Rhaeadr

Pistyll Rhaeadr and Wrexham steeple,
Snowdon's mountain without its people,
Overton Yew Trees, St Winefred's Well,
Llangollen Bridge and Gresford Bells.

Whoever wrote that rhyme of the 'Seven Wonders of Wales' must have come from north-east Wales, because all those wonders are in this corner – with the exception of Snowdon, of course. Clearly the poet was missing out on a few tricks elsewhere, but the one that surely does deserve to be included nationwide is Pistyll Rhaeadr. At the head of a remote valley, the Afon Disgynfa hurls its waters from a lonely mountain plateau some 240 feet (74m) to the valley below. Admittedly the fall is broken at one point, where the water lands in a deep pool to emerge again under an arch of rock, but the whole drop is greater than that that of Niagara! And even if the volume of water isn't in quite the same league, the surrounding scenery is a whole lot prettier!

The walk here takes you first on a balcony path with splendid views of the waterfall before entering a green side valley where lesser falls tumble down the slopes. Overlooked by the imposing ridge of the Berwyns it's a place you are likely to have all to yourself. From there the route goes on to visit both the top and the bottom of Pistyll Rhaeadr, giving you plenty of opportunity to admire it from all angles!

This is a walk on the wild side, possibly at the limit of the scope of this book, but young people will love the adventure of this dramatic landscape, and the magic of the fall itself. Meanwhile, for those who would prefer to do without the ups and downs of this route, a short, easy, and still scenic alternative is on offer.

For the children

- The waterfall itself is exciting. Maybe you will spot the 'Lady of the Waterfall', with a long flowing skirt and hair swept down in front of her face. She lives in there somewhere – look carefully!

- The little waterfalls in the valley are delightful. Children can climb on the rocks alongside and splash their hands in the water.
- A word of caution. Young children will need to be watched carefully at the viewpoint above the falls!

This walk is great in itself, but you still get a Challenge! Can you spot a silhouette of a man walking a dog, a molehill, a sheep dip, yellow lichen on rock, a bat box (a bird nesting box without a hole)? Five out of five earns an ice cream at the café!

THE BASICS

Distance: 3¼ miles (5.25km). Easy route 2 miles (3.25km)

Gradient: Steep climb to top of falls, steep-stepped descent to base

Severity: Moderate/Challenging; with some easy short cuts

Time: 2½ to 3 hours

Stiles: 3

Map: OS Explorer 255, Llangollen and Berwyn

Path description: Grassy track, rough moorland, slippery rock steps on final descent

Parking: Paid parking at café, Grid Ref SJ 076294 or SY10 0BZ. Free on roadside

Toilets: At café

Dogs: Astonishingly, all stiles are supplied with dog gates. But dogs should be on leads in the Open Access Land

Refreshment: At the foot of the falls is Tan-y-Pistyll Café, a rustic establishment serving good food

Start Point: From the roadside parking

PISTYLL RHAEADR WALK

1. From the parking area beside the stream, walk up the road away from the waterfall for about 500m (well beyond the initial rise). Here cross a stile on the bank on the left and bear left on a lovely grassy track with good views of Pistyll Rhaeadr. The track bends right into a side valley where it forks.

2. *For the easy short cut, descend to the left here and cross the stream on a footbridge to reach Point 4.* The main route keeps right at the fork, climbing up the flanks of the valley. *On the skyline is the ridge of the Berwyn Mountains, 2,713 feet (827m) at its highest point.* Cross one stile, then immediately after a second, turn left, descending the  slope beside the fence on your left. The path is not obvious here (and you may have to divert round sedge and gorse) but it becomes clearer lower down. Cross the stream close to the fence to arrive beside a stone sheepfold.

3. Turn right (sheepfold on your left) and walk upstream to a confluence of tributaries. Bear left up the nearest of the tributaries to get a better view of its delightful waterfall. Retrace your steps to the far end of the sheepfold and now go over a metal fence and through the gate alongside. Take the green track ahead and follow it until you see a stile at a fence corner on the right. Cross this and keep ahead beside the wall to rejoin the track. Soon reach a path junction above a wooden footbridge.

4. *The easy route goes straight ahead here, picking up the main route again at Point 5.* The main route takes the right fork, climbing steeply. A waymarker post on the right marks the junction of your descending path. Pass it now and  continue over the hill to another waymarker on the left. Here turn right and go down through the wood to the viewpoint at the top of the falls. *You can only see the water sliding over the ledge and a little spray – to lean out to see the whole fall would be dangerous!* Return the way you came to the first waymarker post and turn right down the steps. After a long descent you arrive at the broad base path.

5. Turn right here and continue through a kissing gate into the wood. Through another gate in the wood you reach the footbridge below the falls – the place for a photograph! Now take the riverside path to the café and return along the road.

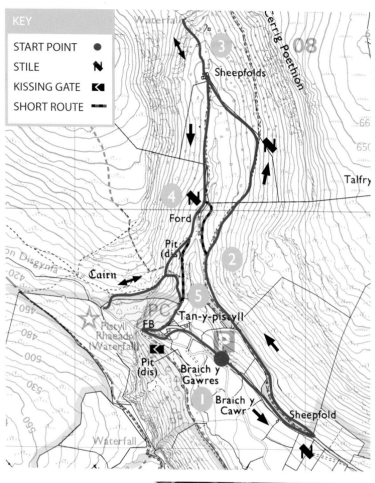

KEY

START POINT ●
STILE 𝐍
KISSING GATE ◄
SHORT ROUTE ▬

Waterfall

Cerrig Poethion

08

Sheepfolds

3

66

650

Talfry

4

Ford

Pit
(dis)

2

on Disgynfa

Cairn

420

5

PC

Tan-y-pistyll

P

460

FB

480

Pistyll
Rhaeadr
(Waterfall)

500

Pit
(dis)

530

Braich y
Gawres

Braich y
Cawr

Sheepfold

550

Waterfall

AKNOWLEDGEMENTS

Thanks go to Eric for his unfailing support during the making of this book.

And then the dedication –

'FOR OUR GRANDSON FREDDIE, A FREQUENT EXPLORER OF THIS CORNER OF WALES'

JUDY SMITH